To Dan —

With hope and certainty that voices found
will continue to swell —

Natasha
Christmas 1991

Rilke and Benvenuta

An Intimate Correspondence

Other Correspondence of Rainer Maria Rilke

Letters on Cézanne

Rilke and Benvenuta

An Intimate Correspondence

Edited by

Magda von Hattingberg
(*Benvenuta*)

Translated by

Joel Agee

Fromm International Publishing Corporation
NEW YORK

Designed by Jacques Chazaud
Printed in the United States of America
First U.S. Edition

Library of Congress Cataloging-in-Publication Data

Rilke, Rainer Maria, 1875–1926.
    [Briefwechsel mit Benvenuta. English]
    Rilke and Benvenuta: an intimate correspondence/edited by Magda von
Hattingberg: translated by Joel Agee.—1st U.S. ed.
        p. cm.
    Translation of: Briefwechsel mit Benvenuta.
    ISBN 0-88064-072-3: $16.95
    1. Rilke, Rainer Maria, 1875–1926—Correspondence.
2. Hattingberg, Magda von, 1883–1959—Correspondence.   3. Authors, German—
20th century—Correspondence.   4. Pianists—Austria—Correspondence.
I. Hattingberg, Magda von, 1883–1959.   II. Title.
PT2635.I65Z487 1987
831'.912—dc19
[B]   87-15660
                                                                                        CIP

Contents

Translator's Note

Feeling has its own syntax, its own connotations and unstandard definitions. I have done my best to preserve both the sense and the sensibility, the literal wording, and the often ambiguous allusions in these letters. (This applies more to Rilke than to Benvenuta, whose messages are rhetorically simpler and more naive, though they accompany his in the same emotional key.) I also thought it important to respect, as completely as possible, the integrity of the sentences, which, at times, especially in the mounting urgency of Rilke's emotions, tend toward what English teachers call the "run-on" effect. (German usage is friendlier to the long breath and the sustained thought.)

A word of thanks: I have been aided inestimably by my friend Lola Gruenthal, who carefully went over the manuscript and whose intuitive grasp of Rilke's thought and language helped me to uncover unsuspected depths of meaning in several especially obscure passages.

Rilke and Benvenuta

An Intimate Correspondence

Benvenuta to Rilke

Vienna
January 22, 1914

Dear friend,

Everything I am writing is perhaps rather foolish and very presumptuous, beginning with the way I address you, for while I am your friend (though without your willing or knowing it), you are not mine, and then there is something else I must tell you: Until now I have never wished to be another person even for a while, until very recently, when the "Stories of God" came into my hands, and I thought it would be beautiful to have been Ellen Key[1] for a very brief time, so that you would know that I love these stories of God "as no one has before." But seemingly foolish things can be said, after all, and so you will perhaps not laugh at me. I also want so much to tell you what warm gratitude I feel toward you and how much you have given to my music. It has long lived within its four walls and now wants to travel in the world in order perhaps to bring a light or a warm good hour to one or another among the many, many people. But when it took its first extended flight into the world, it met with so many bright good eyes and understanding hearts that in its overabundance of unexpected joy, it wants to thank the good spirits who helped it find the way. And so may I thank you too, good spirit; though words cannot speak from the true fullness of the heart. Perhaps, if life should favor me with the chance of finding you somewhere and sometime in the world, Beethoven's word or a very great one by our Sebastian Bach might say it. — For you love music.

I press your hand!

Magda von Hattingberg

Rilke to Benvenuta

Paris, 17, rue Campagne Première
January 26, 1914

Good friend,

Let me take up the rich tone of your letter, it becomes my own nature as I read it; what joy that you wrote it, but how good, too, that you weren't able to turn straight away into Ellen Key—that would have complicated matters excessively. Especially since, from the "Stories of God" on, we were both quite dissatisfied with each other's productions. In the end we wrote one another about it with all the loving rudeness that is justified by a long and thoroughly established friendship.

But perhaps you, too, are indifferent to or displeased with everything I have written since, and now I am supposed to pass on the goodness of your letter, or pass it back, to the highly uncertain address of that young person who, many years ago, rather peculiar years at that, made up stories about the good Lord? What does *he* need it for? I frankly begrudge him the pleasure, it seems to me that he colored in the contours of his feeling in a rather light-hearted spirit, you are giving him much more than he deserves. In truth, though, I cannot tell you anything about him, and perhaps he deserves your gift after all. But no matter how much you spoil him, I have one advantage over him: He will never hear your music, and I do hope that I shall. Now why, if you were traveling, didn't you come through southern Spain[2] last winter? What a reception I would have given you, my heart would have built you one triumphal arch after the other, you would have seen your music perpetually entering without ever arriving, until it reached some innermost place where I myself have never been.

Imagine, I passed that winter in a little Spanish town not far from Gibraltar, I had lived in Toledo for a while, it's easy to write the words, the paper accepts them without complaint— but I assure you, it was not to be compared, it was the Old Testament, it was as if one were imagining it with the whole wealth of the imagination, and yet there it stood every day and every night, every one of those incredible nights. To the same degree that an apparition will surpass the mere bodily presence of a person, this city, this landscape outweighed the existence of landscape as we know it. And one watched, and was with one's whole face beholden to immensity, like Moses. Already in previous years, I had often stood before the greatest impressions of foreign lands; suddenly in Ronda (that place in southern Spain) I realized that my vision was overloaded; there too, the sky advanced so magnificently and the shadows of clouds drew such an expression over the earth — ah, there I sat, and was as if at the end of my eyes, as though one had to become blind now around the images one had taken in, or (granting that destiny and existence are inexhaustible) henceforth receive the world through a completely different sense: music, music: that would have been it. Once, someone played in the little hotel, I didn't see him, I sat in an adjoining room and felt how the world is translated into that wonderful element (I hardly know it, besides it was always too strong for me) with greater abandon, and it gave me an overflowing, almost effortless happiness to feel it coming in from there, for my hearing is new as the sole of a newborn baby.

This I had to tell you, so you may know how things stand between music and me; now I live here, where I have been at home for many years, insofar as I can say this of myself at all, again completely without music, in much inner hardship, for the overabundance of what I have envisioned with such urgency, almost painfully, needs somehow, above all, to be mastered, calmed, and given clean lodging within me. This is what I am wrestling with — but your music lies before me like a season that will eventually come, and if it does not present itself to me here or there, it may happen that I step into its path, the way one goes to Sicily to find the springtime which in the north keeps one waiting and only half hoping.

Your letter reached me today via the Insel-Verlag, I wrote right away, although my stationery had run out, I took this work sheet and wrote, for I do not get to write letters very often these days and the hour was right for this one.

Farewell, dear friend, or rather, welcome, do not let the new dear fire go out, even though now I will only rarely be able to cast in a small grain of heart resin, to make it fragrant for you.

I am affectionately and gratefully yours.

Rainer Maria Rilke

Is the Dr. v. Hattingberg I saw in Munich last summer related to you? Your brother?

᷑

Benvenuta to Rilke

My friend,

How mysterious life is and how strange: One lies awake at night for many hours, tired and sleepless, because of the many fearful visions and pale shadows that will make such a wakeful person long for morning to come, that morning of which one hopes that it will bring something bright, warm, sunny from a great distance as if by a miracle. And before the day has fully emerged from the mists, the front doorbell rings, and there stands the most unmistakable reality: an old gray postman, his beard frosted by the cold. He has a perfectly ordinary-looking envelope in his hand — and yet it is this messenger and none other who brings brightness and heart-warmth from far away: your letter. —

I can hardly say "thank you," because that is hardly an expression for such joy—but since everything we communicate to others must go through the thorny path of language, I say it anyway—thank you from the fullness of my heart. The rest will follow: yes, now I hope that sometime you will "go to Sicily," which in this case is mostly torn out of all geographical context and transplanted to the north, for my path rarely takes me to the south. Genoa and Florence appear in the book of my memories as quite improbably beautiful dreams, Verona too. In the summers I mostly go to a little old village by Lake Garda that I have grown very fond of. But I am afraid this cannot compare with what you describe and the way you describe it!

Years ago, when I was still half a child, I wanted to talk about the nature of music like this, though of course with very different words; probably in the obscure desire adolescents feel, to reveal themselves to another; — people laughed at me and said, by way of comfort: "You are an overwrought little thing" — and I was so ashamed—for the others. And I never spoke about it to them again. But now *you* have come!

Do you know they're all waiting to come to you? The greatest ones of the old times and their disciples and followers — how glad they will be! And how glad I am. Perhaps then, my friend, you will again tell me so beautifully and as only you can, about faraway countries, and fill me with gratitude and happy amazement again and again, as today, when your letter came.

In a few days I will be in Berlin for two or three weeks, then in Munich. Perhaps last summer we walked past one another there without noticing; I spent a long time there, and many weeks in the fall as well. . . .

And now enough for today with this overly long letter. But yours seems to me like a call that requires an echo — therefore you may understand this one.

If your path should sometime take you to Germany, or, in the spring, to South Tyrol, it could happen that we shake hands — in the late fall I may carry out a plan I have entertained for several years and come to Paris — there is a lovely sense of future in the expression: *auf* — but how to put it? *Wiedersehen** is hardly the word. But you will understand!

Many good greetings.

Magda Hattingberg

---

* *Auf Wiedersehen* ("good-bye") literally means "until we see each other again." [Translator's note]

Rilke to Benvenuta

My paper, the stationery, is here now, good friend, but I want to boast and say: it has always been my custom to write to you on this paper I normally use for working, let it remain that way.

It is Sunday, I want to keep it holy by writing to you who now hold such a marvelous future for me in your hands, who have the power to bring upon me wind, storm, and clear weather, the purest vibrations of the cosmos, whichever you choose. My friend, I do not ask when it shall be — it will be. For I never asked, not even when, as a child, I was lost in a military school where life could not even enter, not a single breath of my life. And then everything was there after all, in fact there was always too much, and ultimately all the privations of life come from its abundance. My friend, when you are in Berlin, look at the head of Amenophis the Fourth,[3] in the central glass-roofed court of the Egyptian Museum (I could tell you a lot about this king), feel in this face what it means to be confronted by the infinite world and to counterbalance the whole of it, on such a limited surface, by intensifying the arrangement of a few features. Could one not turn away from a starry night to find in this face the flowering of the same laws, the same imponderable grandeur and depth? I learned to see by looking at such things, and later, in Egypt, when they stood before me in large numbers, surrounded by their own nature, this seeing into them came over me in such waves that I spent nearly a whole night lying beneath the great Sphinx, as if cast out before it from all my life. You see, I have not arrived at music yet, but I know about sounds, and in this connection I had one of the strangest experiences, shall I tell you about it?

You must know, it's difficult to be alone in that place, it has become a commonplace, totally, the most trivial foreigners are dragged to it en masse—but I had skipped the evening meal, even the Arabs were sitting far off around their fire, one of them had noticed me but I managed to get rid of him by buying two oranges from him, and darkness did the rest to protect me from being seen. I had awaited its coming, out on the desert, and then I approached the Sphinx slowly from the back, calculating that behind the next pyramid, which was glowing powerfully in the reddening dusk, the moon must be rising; for there was a full moon. And when I had finally walked around the pyramid, the moon had not only advanced quite far in the sky but was pouring such a flood of brightness over the infinite landscape that I had to dim its light with one hand in order to find my way among the rubble and holes of the excavations. — The Sphinx's hindquarters do not exactly loom significantly over the sandy plain, for since the first excavations the wind has covered it up again several times, and so far, people have rested content with keeping the front part clear up to the paws, so that the ground there, having been dug out, descends toward it as a semi-funnel. By this oblique slope, across from the gigantic structure, I searched for a place to settle and lay there, wrapped in my coat, afraid, in nameless participation. I do not know if I ever became as conscious of my existence as I did during those night hours when it lost all value: for what was it compared to all this? The level on which it took place had receded into darkness, world and existence occurred on a higher stage, on which a star and a god stood adrift in silent communion. You must have experienced this too: that a view of a landscape, of the sea, of a grand, star-studded night inspires us with the conviction of connections and agreements that we are not able to overlook; it was exactly this that I experienced in the highest degree. Here stood a creation that had taken its measure from the sky; upon which the millennia had left no greater mark than a contemptible bit of decay, and the most shocking part of it was that this thing had human features (so profoundly recognizable to us, these features of a human face) and that they were sufficient to it in its exalted position. Ah, dear friend, I told myself, this, this face we alternately hold out to fate and cover with our hands, it must be capable of meaning something great if its form can survive in such an environment. That countenance had acquired the customs of cosmic space; parts of its gaze and smile were destroyed, but indestructible emotions had been mirrored into it by the rising and falling skies. From time to time I closed my eyes, and although my heart was beating, I reproached myself for not feeling this strongly enough; did I not have to arrive at places in my amazement where I had never been before? I told myself: Imagine you had been carried here with bandaged eyes and laid down aslant in this deep, almost impalpably wafting coolness—you wouldn't know where you were, and if you opened your eyes now . . . And when I actually opened them, dear God, — it took them a long while before they could withstand it, before they could take hold of this being, achieve the mouth, the cheek, the brow, on which moon light and moon shadow shifted from expression to expression. How many times my eye had already attempted the ampleness of this cheek; it rounded itself so slowly toward the top, as if in that space there were room for *more* places than here among us. And then, just as I was looking at it again, I was suddenly drawn into its confidence in a most unexpected way, and I came to know it, I experienced it in the most perfect feeling of its roundness. I did not realize *what* had happened until a moment later. Imagine this: Behind the projection of the royal hood on the sphinx's head, an owl had taken wing in the pure depth of the night and slowly, with an ineffable sound, brushed against the face in its soft flight: and now the contour of that cheek was engraved, as if by a miracle, in my hearing, which had become utterly clear after hours in the night stillness.[4]

That, discounting a few exceptions, is what my music was like until now; I was almost afraid of any other kind, unless it was happening in a cathedral, reaching directly up to God, without dwelling on me — and in Egypt I was told, and understood, that in the Ancient Empire music (one suspects) was forbidden; it could only be brought forth before the god; only for his sake, as if he alone could endure the immensity and allure of its sweetness, as if for any lesser being it would be lethal. *Isn't* it, my friend? Do you really know what it is? And already as a child, you were on familiar terms with this and walked about among the lions and angels of this element, secure in the faith that you would not be hurt? Or is music the resurrection of the dead? Does one die by its edge and rise from it shining, no longer destructible? But is my heart strong enough yet to completely die of it, so as to emerge from it whole? You see, I had to form myself from inside out, yielding to the blindness within, for all outer voices were alien, hostile, for many years, and when eventually there came a call in goodness, it would always sound much too vast. I remember thinking, whenever I was on a wide plain, that a man only became a hero because the clouds on a spring evening towered so audaciously above the horizon — but then this was possible too, that a person's life could be ruined because he happened, in passing, to hear a violin, and that tone deflected his entire will toward a denser fate. When I recall the immediacy of impending violence in some interrupted piece of ancient music such as I heard in Italy or Spain, and sometimes in southern Russia—then Beethoven appears to me like the lord of hosts, with power over all other powers, tearing open tremendous dangers in order to overarch them with shining rescues.

Ah, my friend, I'm only dreaming it; some day you will let me experience it, alone with you—; the concepts that do not yet have a name are surely the most futuric and certain, and so what we cannot call a *"Wiedersehen"* will be in the best of hands. But before that (it may take a very long time), *please,* an occasional line, whenever impressions, people, or a book unexpectedly remind you of your friend.

Rainer Maria Rilke

Rilke to Benvenuta

Paris, 17, rue Campagne Première
February 4, 1914

Friend, beautiful heart, how my heart streams, streams toward you — I wish I could write you in one sitting all the possible letters that could be written in a year, you know there are such mornings by the sea, cheerfully strong, all the waves want to come in at once, they linger outside, there's a glistening, glistening, and none comes.

But there is such clear joy between us, so clear that the most distant towns can see one another, and the bells move almost visibly through the receptive air.

My friend, if only you would come — then again, when I imagine us meeting I feel that I am deceiving you: for one, you

11

see, you must accept in the fullest sense what I recently wrote about the limitations of my ear: that it is like the sole of a newborn child: that is to say: not only as new, as unused, as *previous* to any use, but also as clumsy, as useless and awkward and ultimately (as I was assured again and again even as a child) altogether incapable of walking, unable to learn the first three steps. (Truly, I can't recall a tune, not even a song that moved me, that I have heard thirty times over, though I'll recognize it, but I wouldn't be able to tell one note from another—surely this is the most dense incapacity conceivable.) This. — And then another thing. Friend, sister, favorite sister in this unalloyed bliss, you blessed, glad, bright, unrestrainable soul: chance, dear, vivacious chance has urged books upon you that were written a *long* time ago; who was I then? Who am I now? Do I even have a right to open your letters, are they not meant for one who is no longer there, one for whom I myself sometimes feel a kind of nostalgia, if I may put it that way? . . . How would everything have turned out if instead you had read a certain two-volume book of prose, a work in which I expected to draw from a store of old hurts, not realizing that I was just entering upon my inheritance of pain, unspeakable times. Not that I lost my faith in what is most great, not that I grew faint and withdrew, *not any of that,* I did go on, surely. But when I ask myself *how,* my friend, it seems to me that I simply walked into a mountain before me, and the mountain really gave way, and I was able, by means of constant miracles against nature, to go on, inhaling stone and exhaling stone, subsisting in nothing but stone. Now I do not love "miracles" and I take pleasure in nature, so it is not surprising that I sometimes felt monstrous inside my mountain, I became impatient, tired, exhausted: I hoped for someone who would dig me out with a pickaxe, who would chisel me free, who would lay me on a meadow beneath the wind, who would say nothing, who would understand everything, who would be

12

there; ah, probably I screamed so loudly that some passersby really did set about unearthing me, but when they had brought me back to light, these good souls, it was all wrong. I have not had much practice with people, I behaved clumsily with them, in the end I asked them to leave, and no sooner were they gone than I crept back into my mountain, for outside I would so senselessly abandon myself to people, give myself over to them and, for sheer awkwardness, receive nothing in return, while the stone at least held me together and gave me such pure and steady occupation, and it wasn't all equally hard; then my feeling overleaped other people, and I wanted to stay, or, if I was to be saved, it would be by the angel, with *him* I could trust myself to have the right relation. Also, there must be a degree of need to which angels will lend an ear, radiations of extreme anguish that are imperceptible to human beings, that penetrate through their dense world until, beyond, they meet with an angel's brightness and strike a gentle, dolorous note of violet, like amethyst in druses of rock crystal.

Good friend, this needs to be said, *had* to be said: the man who writes to you is much more like the man in this fairy tale (which continues and cannot yet be finished) than that young person of the past whose books you have read and been moved by. This man (to whom no one here is permitted entry) would write to anyone: Do not come. To *you* (his unexpected friend, in whom he has the deepest confidence) he writes: Act, my friend, according to your joy: *It* cannot but do what is right, it has power and glory on its side.

Rainer Maria Rilke

Paris, still the fourth

Good friend, this morning, when I wanted to pour out to you, at once, joy and warning and a thousand other feelings from my innermost being, I neglected to mention the one important and actual thing:

13

That as I am presently established here, there is no chance of making music. I myself have inveighed against the existence of pianos in my presence.[5] There is one standing at my neighbor's, it is not allowed to move, I have vanquished it with my wrath.

And the more I think about it, in the end it seems a good thing that it cannot be *here* and *now*. I have embarked on some undertakings that I must bring to a conclusion in the *same* frame of mind (good or ill, as it may be), for every new tone (I know this) brings other times for other things. So let us not mingle what will be with what is. I have told you about the present, I am still in the middle of it; wrestling, wrestling.

Does this frighten you? Is the one who goes through this in his own way a stranger to you, compared to the one who, coming to you from his earlier books, was permitted to be your friend? This you will write me in your next letter, and it will be addressed wholly to me, to my present self, whether he be understood or denied. But surely all this cannot injure your joy—can it?

Rainer Maria Rilke

(Hastily, as a postscript, toward evening)

Rilke to Benvenuta

Paris, 17, rue Campagne Première
February 5, 1914

Here now is the third letter (since yesterday), my friend. I wired you in the morning, regretting in advance that I would do so, but to tell the exact truth, I *had* to — oh, what am I saying? If truth were the main issue I would have to write you day and night, just to express all the surging and rising and sinking between the contradictions, and even then, God knows whether I could make myself understood, since I myself don't understand it all. And yet, from my very first letter, I have not felt right about burdening you with all sorts of circumstances in my life that are of no concern to you, to make this life important before you and with all these words succeed only in clouding the joy you have borne toward me, pure as the morning breeze that ushers in the spring day. What shall I do?

For months I have been busy hiding, and now that your kindness and joy suddenly seek me out, I behave like a little boy who takes the matter terribly seriously, crying "Not yet! Not yet!" because he wants to hide himself much better first, so that he'll be able, later, to hold on to his utmost shock and delight at being found. — Then again, when I write like this, I seem to myself like a landscape that begs the good sun to please not rise quite yet (yes, I implore the good sun), telling it how long the night has been and how stormy and dark, and that it's a shame, the condition its trees are in.

Who are you, dear friend? This garden is afraid of the sun. That's because it has been so dug up and turned over it no longer looks like a garden, and because once again it is committed solely to becoming, to pure preparation, to regular winter conditions, a pre-becoming beneath a hard harsh ugly surface — not at all fit to receive you, radiant one, nor the god or demi-god who is with you, pressing for results—; imagine if Orpheus had entered the Lord's creation with his infinite lyre before the mountains were quite mountains and the water was quite water; — in the same way I too think my few rocks must first stand solid and my river flow, and my ten trees should first be unmistakable trees to anyone who sees them: Then let the storms of inspiration or divine tranquility do what

15

they will — things beyond comprehension — move them and ravish them. Am I distressing you, friend? No, I couldn't, could I? — in the face of your wonderful joy!

Now I think to myself, what I am recounting and throwing in your path should not, on the other hand, deter you from coming to visit me soon, if you can do so without upsetting your schedule, and if your desire for it remains justified. For besides me, heaven knows, there is Paris, and this much is certain: Paris is incomparably more beautiful in the early spring than in the fall, especially to one who has not seen it before. I will now tell you sincerely how I, in keeping with my solitary soul, would behave. First I would take your hand in both my own and let it rest in them as long as it pleased; but then I would immediately withdraw completely again into my habitual reclusion, undertake nothing and give very little; still, we would have a few afternoons, an evening, a shared walk, all those things which, not having ever been granted us before and hence being few, and rare, would already be very much. We would have immeasurably good things to say to one another, and in the end a future meeting might be agreed upon in a more certain and tangible form, perhaps again guided by that voluminous yellow monster;* for even if it were feasible to find a suitable place and instrument, I have a sense that your music should not sweep over me *here,* in this city which to me is so desperately depleted of life and worn by pain, which has become such a burden to me that I would not even be able to show it to you innocently, beautiful though it is in its singular nature. Your music (thus do I yield to dreams) should not only bring order into my inner world, it should also be associated with new outer relationships. You will say that I am immod-

* Rilke is probably refering to the thick European railway guide and time table with its yellow cover. [Tr.]

erate. I am, my friend, as surely nothing of great urgency is ever moderate, and nature least of all.

Rainer Maria Rilke

(If you would just write that all this has not made you utterly angry at me!)

Rilke to Benvenuta

Paris, 17, rue Campagne Première
February 7, 1914

My friend, I am leaving my work for a moment, giving in to my heart, which wishes it were with you: Your letter of Thursday just arrived, I was afraid to open it, afraid that my telegram* had made you sad, if not angry, and now, dear, you say "glad"; oh, how glad you would be if only you knew what confidence is surging up in me, toward you . . . Friend, can I even describe it to you: so many words come together: All at once it might be too much for you.

You see, what depresses me so greatly about my telegram is this: that it contained a trace, a small trace of retraction, and that it is precisely this gesture which has been my lot in human relations since I was a child: to reverse the urge of an infinite desire to give by an incomprehensible need to take everything back, and whenever this happened in the midst of the rush of

---

* *Rilke's Telegram* to Magda von Hattingberg, February 5, 1914:

PARIS 40352 34 5 9H 58
NO I MUST NOT CALL FOR MUSIC AT ONCE THE MORE I CONSIDER IT TWO LETTERS
ON THE WAY THIRD FOLLOWING SOON DEFINITELY
RMR

feeling—had to happen, with a jolt—it was like dying. And now I don't want to, I *will* not experience it again, not for fear of inflicting and suffering pain, but simply out of truthfulness; for how could I have gotten into this situation if it did not have its deepest root in the fact that I am not true in my devotion? Is it that? The enormous powers that sometimes dwell inside me have taught me a devotion that is without limits: Do I commit the error of transferring to the outer world what ought to be given to these powers only, thus causing inevitable disasters? That is why the saint has such inexpressible significance for me, because *he* alone manages not to cause floods or swamps, nor does he dry out, or ooze away among the rubble, nor need he worry about being navigable — all he has to do is to collect all the pure trickles of his heart, take in a hundred unconscious springs and the affluence of his tears, until, impelled by the ever-growing emotion of his nature, he plunges down God's rocky riverbed, surging, surging in anticipation of the infinite arrival.

How I have longed to be like him. But have I not, by my art, been born closer to the human sphere, shall I turn my life away from it and never know it? Not know it in its simple, innocent comfort, its gentling influence, its tender urgency? Because I can see its movement from afar, the good and complete conjoining of all its members; so long as it doesn't directly concern me, I have a sense of sympathetic attunement and familiarity even with its cruelest features, so that wherever someone happens to let go, I feel that I could carry on where he left off, love it, accomplish it, suffer it — without ever having learned it. But whenever I was committed by or to it, I was paralyzed, found myself incapable, fearfully took back all I had given of myself, whereto I don't know — revoking everything.

If you ask why, I would have to go far back. But ultimately it was always like this, and must have already been this way when I was a child: that whenever my heart was made to feel better and more capable by some human influence, it would simultaneously experience the strangest limitation in its most essential, highest, most blessed use. Work has such strange primordial prerogatives in its claim on this heart; ever since I have come to know it a little, it has belonged to work, and when someone comes and replenishes its lamp with clear oil, so that it lights up with a purer flame and a wider circumference is revealed by its radiance, and loftier images, I ask myself: Does it *have* to be this way, that the other now wants all this greater beauty and brilliance for himself? Perhaps this is the way it's supposed to be, perhaps one just has to choose — and yet, Nature does not act like this; when she glorifies a heart, she wants nothing for herself; and night, when she descends on a heart with her strong stars, wants nothing for herself. And when music magnifies a heart a thousandfold — am I not right? — music does not want anything for itself. My God, music; you can believe there were moments when I hoped for it — imagining again and again that among the powers of the earth there must be *one* that would connect me to all that is human without my suffocating in it, one that would bring my heart to flower indescribably and then hedge it about with a space of protection and allowance, to let it bring forth the true fruit which it has never borne. Ah, my friend, what am I doing, what am I doing? When I reread your first letter: how simple it was, how dear, and light — is it wrong of me to drag in all these difficult things instead of simply keeping my peace, just being, and waiting to see what God and you will do for me— —?

Rainer Maria Rilke

Benvenuta to Rilke

Vienna
February 6, 1914

Oh dearest—I have your letter and have read it again and again and held it in my hands as if its many pages were your hands.

Believe me, I knew all of this, or rather, I felt it—*all* of it, and today, when I actually experienced it, I did something I haven't known how to do for a long time: I cried.

Look, my brother, there has been unspeakable pain and suffering in my life, and even now, so much bitterness and darkness comes into my days. But the great joy you sensed in me is an unchanging possession within me, in spite of everything; again and again, this joy opens its eyes and tells me it will not die as long as I live. But it is this joy you are still afraid of, my brother — it is music, but not just the music that reveals itself in sounds; it is like that good spirit of an unknown, heavenly kindness that fills our ears and our souls in the thousand vibrations and the gentle breathing of nature, especially at those moments when we need her most — ". . . and there was such assurance in her, as if she had known for years that she would have to begin at this moment . . ." Do you really believe that I don't know Brigge and this beautiful passage in it? And do you think I don't know what is written between and above the words?

No, I am not only fond of the young person who wrote books many years ago, I also know the man who lives deep, deep inside the rock — I love him too, perhaps him especially — and I want to bring him out from the rock; the thought does not scare me, for he will not say: "Leave"; no, he won't, for he already has that loving trust that says: "Act, my friend, according to your joy; *It* cannot but do what is right . . ." —

It was only the other, faint-hearted feeling that made you say: No, not yet! Do overcome it, my dear, dear friend, and don't be afraid of what my joy wants to bring you. It will not hurt you and not be disappointed by what you call your incapacity. Perhaps we can remove the hard stones layer by layer with some hard work. But you shall feel how delightfully the wind comes across the meadows with the fragrant greeting of distant silent cool pine woods — and how the white daisies bow and sway in the high soft grass; the dear little bellflowers, too, with their deep violet color: They would like to sound the music's soft first notes. Don't you trust your ear to understand such a gentle beginning? And to learn, by imperceptible transitions, to bear the ever more powerful and radiant waves of sound? Until you reach those wonders you have not even imagined yet. Are you still afraid of it?

How much I have to tell you, and how narrow is the frame! How many hours would be needed just to get past the beginning; you are so right when you say that one would like to write immediately all the letters one could write in a year.

But is it not a blessed thought to know that everything still lies before us? Securely sheltered in the future. And the more trustingly we wait for it to come, the more beautiful it will be.

I am now reminded of a great experience: It was on an evening; I was at the Vienna Opera, sitting somewhere high up on an inexpensive seat among people who were neither beautiful nor elegant, with work-worn hands and modest clothes; it was warm and no one was talking, for the souls of all these people, tired from their day's work, were silently waiting: *Die Meistersinger von Nürnberg* was being presented.

Suddenly darkness fell and the narrow head with the hard

features rose in the orchestra pit: Gustav Mahler. Then he rose altogether and stepped up to his place on the podium — he raised his hand with the baton — a moment in which one seemed to be hearing the throb of one great heart — and I almost thought I would faint. The hugeness of that moment: Not a single sound lost yet and the whole glory still ahead—; of course the bliss of that radiant upward rush in C major that suddenly flooded over all hearts together cannot be described in words.

I was very young then; later (three years ago now) I experienced something similar, even more consciously, when I heard *Parsifal* for the first time in Bayreuth. . . .

The day demands its labors, I have to go, but I will continue writing soon.

In the afternoon

Your second letter just arrived; oh the doubts and fears your heart is wrestling with! Everything, everything I have told you today should dispel them, my dear, dear . . . if you have the time and inclination, I would like to send you a book called "Outline of a New Esthetics of Music," and it is written by the man who—I'm tempted to say—revealed and taught me that sounding world, Ferruccio Busoni. I am sure that only a very few have so perfectly expressed the nature of music in words. I have known Ferruccio since I was a child and have experienced many glorious things thanks to him; my purest and grandest impressions have come to me through him, directly and indirectly. . . . If you would like the book, I shall send it soon. You will love and understand it—it is written by a very great human being.

Farewell, until the next farewell and the next hour of beautiful communion.

M.

Rilke to Benvenuta

Paris, 17, rue Campagne Première
February 8, 1914

Oh my sister. Precious one, are you* there, is it possible, has God given you to me in the years of my life's anguish, that I may survive? Am I permitted to feel the world, breathe its air, certain that it contains *you,* my new-found friend, as I know that God is contained in it, whom I know, whom I have experienced as boundlessly in the bliss of my work as you have in your music? Dear heart, I have not asked anything of God for a long time (I do not ask him for my art, we have too much mutual pride for that: He will have to throw it into my heart, if he can't desist—), but now I *beg* him to let me love you, Benvenuta, with all the roots of my heart, so that this love may benefit you, beautiful heart, that it may entertain your joyousness within you, that it be the garden of the wonderful season you are whirling toward me, immortal joy; that it be a garden: because a garden does not make an effort to bloom, it takes pleasure in blooming, it finds itself resting in every flower; oh sister, what have I done, that love always came to me as a thing to *achieve,* that I have never borne its sunny fruit through my nature, as an orange tree bears its innocent, blissful abundance; that I had to go to and fro with it like a slave in the marketplace,[6] carrying my load of provisions that I could not see, which the god purchased over my head to use for his feasts that I could not attend?

Children *rest* in love (was I ever allowed that?), but then

* Here, for the first time, Rilke addresses Benvenuta with the familiar *Du.* [Tr.]

23

they are still pure in their illusion that it is possible to belong to someone; and when they say "mine," they make no claim to ownership; they hug and let go, and when they do hold on, it is God with whom they are still dimly enmeshed, who draws the others to himself through these innocently open arms.

Can you* explain (the "Du" I suddenly felt shall not rob me of the earlier word, I want to say *everything* to you, call you by every name, and thus keep alive the feeling that to me you are closeness and distance, that you are openness and at the same time a refuge from that openness); can you explain it, friend, why people have such fateful influence upon me? I shall confess to you that if my neighbor were to enter now—a young Hungarian painter whom I scarcely know and for whom I have no feeling beyond the sympathy one has for young people when one is no longer convinced of one's own youth—no more than that—if he were to enter, he would not be able to even guess *what* it is that consumes me, but I would put aside my pen and for two hours, until I ran out of breath, relate impressions and memories with the warmth (can you imagine this?) that belongs to *you,* that goes out to you from here, with this embezzled warmth and none other — what in the world is that? Certainly not kindness: a weakness, a sickness, vanity, a crime? . . . And I do the same thing with my work: The innermost tension that is there for its sake, to which it alone has a claim, finds release in some trivial occasion, expends itself, dissipates in the air: Must I not, then, shut myself off, as the merchants do their attar of roses? And, my dear, that would only be right, wouldn't it? Why not say: I want to be alone? Wasn't *he,* Beethoven, alone for the sake of his music, and in the loss of his hearing was he not bereft of his last hold on any kind of otherness, so that he would become like a forest in the

* Here he reverts to the formal *Sie.* After several alternations, he eventually settles for *Du.* [Tr.]

primeval roar of its silence and no longer know that it is possible to be that other who hears the forest and is afraid? My friend, believe me, this is *all* I want. And in the same breath with which I ask God to let me love you without reserve, I beg, I implore him to give me the strength, the will, the desire for the most militant solitude, for in my whole being there is no place that is not destined for it. Oh do you feel it, sister, do you feel it in your brother's heart when you hold your hands against it, the nameless urge to push everything aside, all tenderness, and to go the hard, the splendid path of action, from deed to deed, irresistibly? Do you feel it? And that in the end there would be no need to prepare a funeral pyre for me, that I myself would have set my perfected heart on fire with the flame of my rapture, to let it consume itself utterly and flare up in a single flame to God.

But, Benvenuta, here I am, locked in, you see, behind my door, and do not act. How often, in nature, have I watched a little bug attempt something, and fail, and try it again and again — you see, I would say to myself, he too is alone. How easily God could help him climb this stalk, and it isn't really that God doesn't *want* to—but he knows the bug would be frightened if he helped him, the bug might give up everything and think, I feel so peculiar, as if everything had changed, as if I weren't a bug any longer— Thus God takes heed and keeps himself far away from the little creature, but I suspect that each time the little creature resumes its ascent, it no longer knows anything about its last disappointment and defeat, has forgotten everything, stands again before something completely new, quite eager to find out what will happen this time, full of cheerful enterprise. In the past, if I'm not mistaken, it seemed to me every morning, or at least now and then, as if each beginning were the first, the only one, and now, for a long time, it has been the opposite. The least and the greatest I set myself to

25

accomplish, even things that are perfectly dear and close to me (and perhaps especially those) are burdened in advance by such an indescribable load of experience and suspicion of incapacity. In the morning, when I lay out my work before me, often just an empty page of stationery, I am already flooded by this anticipation: You won't be able to do it; and often I can't. The decisive element in art, what people have long called "inspiration," is of course not at our disposal, but *that* I have always understood: that it couldn't be otherwise, given our unreliable nature; it never troubled me, I never used the least means to stimulate or invoke it — to be patient with the divine is so natural, for it has other standards. My trouble comes from another side and has but slowly spread its infection to where my true certainties lie. A young, slightly eccentric French author (I would like to send you his book—his name is Marcel Proust[7]—the same copy over which I have spent my evenings, with a few pencil markings) speaks of a peculiar fear which during his childhood carried great importance and exerted a strong influence upon him. In the later course of his life, when there could be no more question of his having such a fear, he believed he still recognized it in different guises, c'est cette angoisse qui revient dans l'amour. If that can be true, mine is the next phase, l'angoisse de ne pouvoir pas aimer qui revient dans le travail.

My dear friend, so you did know Brigge. He and I are separate, of course, yet he took a lot into his life that was mine, some of it almost completely — but what a record that would be, if the inexpressible sufferings of the past three or four years were precipitated in written words. The rift in my heart dates only from certain other events—that rift which must be the reason why there is such an ambiguous fluttering whenever nature, whenever lofty things, when the stars, touch upon it. (You should have heard it earlier — sister, what exaltation, when, purely touched, it sounded forth such purity—). That was on a great voyage to another continent:[8] I had opened my heart wide to the mightiest things, and at the same time, since it was so exposed, such fatefully distorted conditions invaded it. My profound receptiveness, offered up to the highest, became saturated with guilt and torment, I lost all my bearings, all assurance, except for that place in my heart that has always remained a home to me in all vicissitudes. I remember a night in a small hotel room in a Tunisian town; the alien horror of my surroundings had penetrated so deeply into my own nature that I seemed to be touching myself with hands that were not my own. There was no electric light, I lit a candle, I sat on my bed — my friend, try to understand: this simple little flame, into which I must have often drowsily gazed as a child, will you believe me: It was the first thing in a long time that I knew and recognized — a dear survivor of an earlier, lost world, *my* world, can you understand that, I felt an emotion toward it, a swelling gratitude, something like what I now feel toward you.

"Not a single sound lost yet and the whole glory still ahead—" how I understand that, dear heart! And to think that *this* is how one used to stand before life — and now, what losses, and *ahead* . . . ?

My loving friend, you see, my life was never given a foundation, no one was able to imagine *what* it would want to become. In Venice there stands the so-called Ca del Duca, a princely foundation, on which later the most wretched tenement came to be built. With me it's the opposite: the beautiful arched elevations of my spirit rest on the most tentative beginning, a wooden scaffolding, a few boards . . . Is that why I feel inhibited in raising the nave, the tower to which the weight of the great bells is to be hoisted (by angels, who else could do it)? — During the past two years I have read a lot of Goethe, to whom for a long time I had felt no real attraction; now he becomes important to me, indeed moving in his humanity, which I was least prepared for, and again and again I admire the way he steadily built upon his foundations with such splendor and control, limiting himself at the very top only because that was the spirit in which his pyramid needed to be completed. How wonderful all this is, how wonderful are great lives, how wonderful yours is to me, precious friend! A life to which I suddenly speak as though I were addressing the cloud banks and depths of my sky, to discuss when and where to supply my nature with showers and clear weather. — What an overwhelming sweep, each night, from sky to earth. When I open the window into my bedroom (next door is the high studio where I live and work) — how I have to compose my face first, to make it adequate just to the nearest star. What a mighty sweep from feeling to spirit, what freedom in the soul, what overpowering emotion from one human being to another.

Tomorrow evening you will be in Berlin. Perhaps the letter I wrote you yesterday afternoon—it went off to Vienna first (registered)—will be awaiting you there. This one I won't be able to post until tomorrow morning, my little post office takes Sunday seriously and will not be receptive until tomorrow. — Farewell, dear true friend, champion on behalf of my future, joyous and beautiful heart, sister, farewell. Tell me soon how it is for you in Berlin. Many of your paths are familiar to me; I lived in Schmargendorf for years, in a small house that has probably long disappeared, it went by the name of Villa Waldfrieden.[9] That is where I wrote the Stories of God, intermittently crossing the road (this was still possible then), barefoot, into the rural Dahlem forest, where there was no one besides me and the trusting deer.

R.M.R.

(Yes, pictures. Yours, may I have it soon? Here are three small ones of me, though I doubt whether you can decipher them.[10] But there are no others: I have not allowed any to be taken for some ten years, partly because I don't like the modern, self-important, "independent" sort of photograph (*old* photographs all the more)—partly because the indiscreet publicity of our time will all too readily use any given picture for the silliest sort of commerce. — Last summer, finally, a friend who was quite intent upon such an endeavor succeeded in taking the three little pictures.)

(As for Busoni's book, I would like to devote some quiet hours to it, if I may have it from you — and if you have time for Proust's "Du côté de chez Swann," I will send it to you shortly.)

Benvenuta to Rilke

Last day Vienna
February 7, 1914

I was in a fairytale world of hoar frost — took a long beautiful walk while reading today's greeting from you; and imagine, I laughed for joy — so that the jackdaws, startled and offended, took flight from their trees with insulted expressions on their faces. I really laughed and thought: Oh you stupid, foolish garden, don't you know that the sun has to come and go according to eternal laws — even if the land is covered by mist, the sun is still there and each night conceals a new dawn. Dear—dear little boy who is hiding (may I speak this way?)—there once was someone who very gravely and seriously said—"even though now I will only rarely be able to cast in a

29

small grain of heart resin—" Has this not become the most deliciously inconsequential remark? And does not everything one could almost call "theory" turn to naught before the gold of reality?

There stands my big valise, its angry jaws wide open, jealous of the inkwell's incredible prerogatives. The inkwell's all puffed up with pride, as weighty in its arrogance as the neglected thing that wants to be finally packed. I have to attend to it, otherwise it might, in its malice, contrive to get lost on the way to Berlin. That would be a pretty tale! But now the inkwell's annoyed. If one could only please everyone!

I will write more from Berlin. You must take today's high spirits at face value. And believe and know and be glad as well, my dear —

A thousand dear thoughts.

M. H.

Rilke to Benvenuta

Paris, 17, rue Campagne Première
February 9

Dear bright sun, go on, laugh — why indeed shouldn't you? But your little boy is very much afraid of you, and this may have to do with the fact that his playing hide-and-seek isn't just an exuberant invention: he must have been up to a great deal of mischief the last few years, and had finally to crawl off into a corner, rather in earnest—yes, that must be it.

February 10, early

I wrote this quickly yesterday, when your letter came, surprising me (I hadn't expected to receive another one from Vienna) — then I had to let it go, divided, not between luggage and inkwell but between this sheet and another one that sent its complaints of neglect from the work desk to the writing table, reminding me constantly of its privileges, one after another. Incidentally, I would have taken sides with your suitcase, you can't imagine how mine intimidates me; when I consider how involved we have been with each other these past years — I know all its habits, but it ignores mine, eight days before I depart from somewhere I can already discern what its mood will be and whether it will make my life difficult. I have more dealings with it than with all the other things that consider themselves my belongings, and yet ours has remained a relationship based on respect, in which I play the subordinate part. If I were to address my valise, it would have to involve a title, but we communicate with signs—many small ones, on my part, while his consist of a few large general gestures over my head.

Dear, dear soul, sometimes I am so moved by the fact that you are there. This morning I got up, I talked to you, as if you were all there is. My sister, dearest, I don't even have a picture of you, and can't imagine or guess what you look like — I only see you walking beneath the hoar frost, a dear distant figure. Hoar frost, how long it is since I've seen any; once in a patch of Swedish winter many years ago, we were driving in a sled through a landscape completely oppressed by a radiant burden — but to *walk* there is almost more beautiful, to *feel oneself walking* in that great pure soundlessness; let us do it together sometime and take it upon ourselves, the two of us, to insult the jackdaws with our irrepressible gaiety.

". . . that worries are a mistake," as Goethe's mother so nimbly put it, according to Bettina, yes yes, the starry sky stands there every night proclaiming the law, worries *do not exist* if one measures them against this, there are none in music, none in my poems, and yet my heart is replete with worries.

Dear Magda, accustom yourself to seeing my heart, it is not so easy, believe me; there are friendly cordial people who like me in my books, that is one thing; they come to me with expectations they have formed by reading me, fine, wise, and pure expectations, how could I disappoint them, no, I don't do that. But you see, my books are telescopes; when someone looks in, all sorts of things fly through his vision: skies, clouds, objects, apparitions, who knows what, all suspended in a brave deep openness, more powerful, singular, and valid than anything he is used to; very well, let him enjoy it, but all this is not me. Only *you* know this—am I not right? Take a good look through the well-aimed telescope, there's a small bright spot—do you have it?—*that* is my heart, you can't make it out. Ah, my sister, is it a house? Is it just a bright rigid place in the rock, blindly blinking through the cheerful green of an active and bustling nature? — —

(Don't be alarmed, I will say "*Sie*" to you countless times, but not "*Sie*" and "sister" together, that sounds as if I were very ill and you had taken on the task, complete with uniform, of nursing not just me but whoever may come.)

Later

The femme de ménage came in to clean up—very late; every morning she comes with her store of gossip newly replenished — it never occurs to her that one might not feel like listening. And so one allows oneself to be watered for a while,

like a potted flower, trusting in nature's well-known magna-
nimity that somehow this humidité will also help one to grow,
hélas, chère amie — how all these minor characters whom
one admits to make the irksome business of the day soundless
and smooth, themselves become a new noise, an obstacle, a
definite discomfort! Isn't it as if one were buying rugs only to
tumble over them in every conceivable way? In short, I did what
I do every morning—I ran away, after having been sufficiently
watered.

Still later

Time and again, good friend, and now too, I feel uneasy, as
though I were deceiving you. My descriptions must lead you to
believe that I am badly off; but if you came in here and looked
around, you would find that, with some common sense, it
should be possible to have an excellent life here. And when I
speak of the bagnio of the last few years, there were, after all,
the great voyages; and whenever I came back, overwhelmed
by their surfeit of both good and ill, old friends outdid one
another in finding me quarters to live in, which were grander
the more diminished they found me. The splendors I have
been surrounded by, my favorite sister, you would not believe
it. And even now, as I endure this Paris, which has become so
unproductive and onerous for me — the bounty that is at my
disposal without my even having to ask — country houses,
castles, parks — where, at my convenience, I could set up
house all by myself, looked after by familiar servants who
consider me part of the family. . . . You see, every time I
seized one of these great opportunities, it turned into something beautiful, certainly, and it did not fail to yield some rich
rewards, and yet when I left, I always felt that I had somehow
wasted it, more or less the way a dog will waste the wonderful

gray or rose of its pillow, no matter how thoroughly it presses its muzzle into the cloth—the inner connection is lacking. There was a present brimful of abundance, inhabited by a past for which one had sufficient imagination and inclination to adopt it for a while, but when one finally let go of the whole thing, it would spring back like a branch full of fruit one had drawn to oneself, and there one stood just as before. Everything had been present in splendid profusion, too much on all sides — but isn't the main point, really, to be surrounded by those few things one needs for the sake of the profoundest task, *those things alone,* arranged as if into a constellation by an ineffable necessity? "Wondrous being," I would have said even a year ago, if suddenly a fairy had appeared before me to grant me a wish, "give me a year of life in *my own* circumstances, none but the calm, calculable circumstances of my work, it won't spoil me, I want to become strong in it for all the unrest I have yet to experience. — Don't children endure the most violent upheavals only because they live in their needs and gratifications, never knowing or even suspecting *the possibility* of a change bursting in on them?" The good fairy does not need examples — she would never have waited this long, my speech might have been much shorter, I sense so well now just *what* is needed for my work. A little bit of real protection (perhaps a great great deal) is needed, because I live my days in a state of receptivity that can be alerted by a ten-thousandth part of a hint, and that every day seduces me to adopt at least forty different existences, not one of which confirms the validity of what I may have begun in another. Just for a while, to have a sameness about the soul, an invariable goodness, a safety, such as is granted a patient in the fresh air, to restore the confidence of his bewildered body. The same days, the same nights, gently summoned from their hesitations by the voice of work. Oh my child, to be permitted to move back and forth between nothing but the darkness your hands could prepare for me and the eternally brilliant space that arises from their music.

Fabulous creature, fairy tale of my heart, don't be alarmed when I let myself be drawn into talking like this, don't conclude that some tangible hope or claim on you is meant by it, there is none, none — also, I know so well that you, especially you, only give what you *have had* to give, from the beginning of time. Have you ever visited a prisoner? — this much one must grant him, that he boundlessly confuses the life outside—wherever it calls to him and before he has seen it—with his own life, the one he has given up—; then this too passes, until he is at peace and alone again with the spider in its gray corner, lost in admiration for the infinite wholeness he sees in it.

But if this troubles you, put me abruptly back, my wholehearted friend, where you want me to be — I have been prepared for such unspeakable pain, what harm could it do me if now, within this bright joy, I have to take a few steps backward?

Before going to sleep

Dear heart, it's evening now, a great full moon, almost stronger than my greenly subdued lamp, is working its way through the open studio window; I used to be able to spend the evenings writing away, now fatigue overcomes me before I even realize it, an immensity of sleep awaits me. That is good, I trust sleep, almost as much as I trust you; it is thanks to sleep that my nature, spoiled though it is, or wilted, in so many places, is still connected to something deep, unused, and darkly innocent.

The eleventh, early

Come to think of it, sisterly friend, how many unfavorable things I would have to tell you, in order to properly prejudice you against me. All that I perceive as bad in myself and cannot overcome, all the falseness, pettiness, meanness, and crudeness in my soul that others have proven to me when they had come to the end of their longest patience, and especially this, the crudeness, for I feel as though I could hear inside me a voice I've known from my earliest childhood that cannot get over the fact that there is this crudeness inside me and that it could strike out blindly . . . as if someone had told me then: You, René, *you* who sometimes are able to sense the coming of the most gentle, subtle, airy things: *how could you* . . . My friend, I don't know who said that first, it would be horrible if some day you were to think something even vaguely like it; that I am capable of it is certain, I have seen it with my own eyes—capable of being clumsy, heavy, brutal (to call it by its name), and *that* in vibrant, soaring realms where brutality no longer exists, where it rises up like a ghost and stares one in the face even as one refuses to believe it. You see, they had convinced me so utterly of the existence of this monstrous fault that I have at times tried to observe calmly where it may come from. It is *this,* I told myself: that, given the enmity I have presumed people feel toward me, I learned affection and intimacy, not from people, but from a few things that sacrificed themselves, so that in the end I had no real judgment about what it is to hurt or be kind to another. For similar reasons, after all, children are capable, in the midst of the gentlest banter, of twisting one's finger nearly out of its socket, because they have developed their heedless affections on dolls, which never talk back. And yet, when I then take stock of my dealings with things, I find that I'm not really fair toward them either. It may be unavoidable that in the presence of a man who lives by himself, many things will fare badly and perish, simply because he just wouldn't know how to help them. But even among those objects I hold especially dear, I see this or that one languishing in a reproachful manner, as if the little roots it has sunk in my mind had struck upon a stone of lovelessness at the bottom and were now dying with a twisted gesture of mute lamentation. It happened once that such a moment's fright arose between myself and a little picture, I felt it like a stab in the middle of my heart (I guess I was supposed to experience it more keenly this time). I basically don't like to own anything, but among the few things that would have no place to stay if they weren't attached to me is a fine colored daguerreotype of my father.[11] It had been made in a hurry for his old mother when, at seventeen, in the penultimate year of his service in the Cadet Corps, he signed up for the war with Italy — (those first naive photographs were capable of such touching truthfulness — this one really shows, as if one were seeing it once and for all through the eyes of his mother, the young, handsome face in the earnest, almost imperceptibly smiling presentiment of unimagined adventures —); I must have seen it once among my father's papers when I was a child, later it was as if lost for years, it was no use asking about it. Then one day I found it as I went through his estate, framed in ancient faded red velvet in the manner of miniatures, unhurt, and of course I realized at the moment of recognition how profoundly it had been grafted into my heart. On closer scrutiny, a few tiny metal green specks became visible near one of the eyes, as though something were corroding the plate. Concerned that the condition might deteriorate further, I had a case made, lined inside and outside with black suede, to shut out completely any further effects of the light. Occasionally I asked for the opinion and advice of people who seemed to know about such things — oh, my dear one, need I tell you the rest? — all this, all this just so that suddenly, again years later, at a time of complete unpreparedness, I would rip open the back of the frame and hurriedly try to correct matters with a wretched wad of cotton, of course aggravating the timid little defect to the point of real destruction . . . A nervousness, a clumsiness, but translate it for a moment into the invisible, the emotional, the spiritual sphere — and you will be uncertain *which* angel to implore on behalf of one who could act both this way and that, who is capable of trampling his own inner-most prudence like a hostile stranger.

Toward evening

Then a letter came, I saw the stamp — still Vienna, I hadn't expected it, though I felt you would have to assuage some difficult, rebellious days; felt it and went on to write you all sorts of confused stuff about me, my friend, instead of—without even knowing it—hitting upon those few words (by an accident of this heart you have so moved) that might have given you comfort, much the way animals are sometimes able to when they cavort and play before one, profoundly guileless within their fate. But if you at least knew, Benvenuta, you who have come to me, whenever a note from you gets here (the last one was beautiful, written out of a single encompassing spirit, as if by moonlight — when the moon is out again I will read it by the window in the night-dark room), when such a letter comes, Benvenuta, if you could only see me descending the stairs with my full, full heart, my teeth pressed into my lower lip, the way children look when they carry a fearfully full cup.

For three days there was a touch of spring in the air here, then last night the full moon came and kept the universe wide open, a cosmic coldness streamed in, today there's a breezing, a clouding, that doesn't quite know what the rules are — we still have to wait. Spring, springtimes — the ones in Paris used to be (how often I have to employ this expression) among the most marvelous I knew; often in the most magnanimous countries my emotion would yearn for Paris, when April came I would stand distracted in front of the orange trees and think— no, breathe—of Paris. Spring in a landscape is easy, but spring in a city— I know only two that are capable of it, for whom spring is their own condition, as if it were bursting out of their bride-pale walls everywhere, as if their windows first caught the invisible groom with their mirrors and then threw him into the near and palpable world (Rome takes him to its great heart, Rome is moved, Rome gives a feast, Rome, when he comes across the Campagna, is already worn out from so much feeling — Rome takes him in as the father welcomes the prodigal son), but I know of only two cities that are so permeated with spring that there is not a place in their pavement, in their facades, even in the suddenly no longer cold railing of the bridges, that has not received the secret knowledge of spring, that will not have a ready reply to the slightest question in the air tomorrow, not one, not a single one failing to recite the whole poem without any mistakes — Moscow, which admits spring as a peasant child admits the story of creation it has learned by heart — and Paris, Paris, which throws its springtimes into the eyes of the light like the pollen of all the love that has delighted and spent itself here since the days of Abelard. Today the spring that holds the most feeling for me is the one I had first experienced in southern Italy and which I stood facing in the southern Spanish mountain landscape exactly one year ago, in nameless emotion. There, where the sun is present all winter, not just as an image, but with virtually undiminished intensity, it imparts not so much a knowledge of

irrevocably good news (one even observes without great pleasure the progress of a few small almond trees and the growing
boastfulness of the sky) — but let just one mild overcast day
come along unexpectedly, hear the *added* feeling, from early
morning on, in the sounds of the birds, how they have become
darker and stand out almost gravely, purely painting themselves into the balmy silence; step outside: with a protective
softness almost like the kind you know from the inside of your
eyelids, grayness rests upon your eye, almost like sleep; and
only then does the color rose that has come to fuller bloom on
the trees overnight seem a miracle, because it is *strong* against
the rain's inconspicuous, diffident presence, strong out of
blissfulness (not extravagant at all); and now stand where you
can see it with the earth as its background: our own heavy,
prepared, laborious earth: this way, too, the rose color is still
strong — differently, the way one is strong when one doesn't
want to cry.

(Passage from my notebook, written a year ago in Spain, facing
the almond trees):

> The almond trees in bloom: all that we can accomplish here
> is to recognize ourselves without residue in the manifestations
> of nature.
> Unending is my amazement, blissful ones, at your behavior, /
> bearing such transient display with everlasting intent. / Ah, one
> who knew how to bloom: his heart would be far beyond any /
> weaker calamity's reach, and in the greatest, serene.[12]

(And a few days later, this):

> The little birds in the evergreen oaks, no longer speaking
> prose, are already making poetry. The heart of one of them,
> bubbling already like a light spring. Where does it come from,
> the tenderness of creatures? — Leaning against a stone: to use

this as an event. To believe in it. — Gathered marsh marigolds by the brook, almost green, a bit of very new yellow painted into the calyx at the last minute. Inside around the stamens, an oil-drenched circle—as if they had nibbled some butter. Green odor from the tubular stems. Finding its residue on my hand, feeling of kinship. Little girl friends, when I was a child, with their hot hands . . . was it this that touched me so? . . .

February twelfth of this year

Joyous friend, my confidante, how much there is that I want to make real for myself in you, in your heart. Childhood — What was it, really? What *was* it, this childhood? How else to inquire about it than with this perplexed question — what was it—that burning, that amazement, that endless insufficiency, that sweet, that deep, that radiant feeling of tears welling up? What was it? How the words I read in St. Augustine (at the time of the Rodin book) went through me: "Where should it have gone?" Could it really still be there inside us, the childhood that had nowhere to go, away from us? But then it vanished so deeply inside us and we turned away toward the things of the world, and now we stand about with such foreignness crowding our faces, and ask: What was it? When we lived it, we did not know it, we used it up, we didn't know its name; and yet it was then we possessed it completely, inexhaustibly; later the things turn up with names, are forbidden to pass beyond them, and, out of sheer caution, leave them half empty. Or else they step out of them and we, thinking this is fate, flee to some meaningless mountaintop as if from the deluge, yelling at one another that the flood is rising. There was a time, long before coming of age, when we lived *everything,* I believe we lived dread to the limit, the utmost dread, we didn't know it was dread; Joy, to the *limit,* never suspecting there could be a joy that was too rich for our hearts (we trembled with it, but accepted it as it was) — and perhaps *love* to the limit as well.

41

(When I consider that I ever *knew* it — when did I unlearn it?). Playmates of my childhood, girls, did I not love you? How I rushed to meet you — and you too were breathless, your hot fragrance rising toward me like midsummer fields of clover — and then we stood far apart, but the ball brought it to me from your hands, in an arc, the loveliness that was half your bodies' and half your souls' incandescence. And when you came, on the birthday afternoon, were *supposed* to come (and this supposed-to-come seemed to be unaccountably prearranged in the order of things — supposed-to-come, at four o'clock, "preferably a little earlier"—), how my room was cleaned up for you, how my dolls sat there, amazed — how the door-knobs glistened. How could I not have loved you? And then other, already grown-up girls one had ignored, counting them among the general run of adults; but one day they were a little less talkative than usual, one could quietly observe them at the coffee table, the most silent one sat across from me — how beautiful she was, one could feel that her hair was no longer a child's hair, cleanly tended by loving hands, yet still the hands of another: no, now it was *her* hair, slightly mysterious even to herself, and probably she loved it—; suddenly one asked one-self, God knows why, whether she might not have recently cried? And already one's heart was reaching out to her across all the cakes and cookies. Did she feel it? Hardly. It was a very one-sided occupation, loving such a big thoughtful girl, one laid one's cheek against the edge of the table on which she had leaned, it was hard. When one saw her in the street, coming around the corner, recognizable from afar in all the disguises of her loveliness, indeed anticipated with one's whole body even before she came around the corner with her French governess — blessed Teresa of Avila, could love's arrow have pierced your heart more imperiously than the dazzling silver point of this fulfillment entering into that swooning pre-sentiment? — Noble passion of troubadours, submission

42

in service — how you took hold of me — first pride of chivalry, first melancholy — that she would never know about it: beautiful feelings, worn one over the other like armor over a pale rose silk doublet. And while the people around one developed worry wrinkles from the effort to protect one against the slightest cold, there was not a place in oneself, day or night, that did not long to die for her.

Did any of them sense it? What became of them? — One of them knew. This I won't forget. It was in the summertime, in a small Bohemian spa. Her name was Hueber, Fräulein Hueber (of course I knew her first name too), but her family name, which I only just realized I remember, had the special charm of having to be pronounced, not Hüber, as one might have supposed, but Hu-eber, and regardless of whether that sounded pretty or not, I found it enchanting. By the way, I have no clear image of her; someone slender and blond flees, half averted, through my memory; I have also completely forgotten how she behaved during that certain scene (a trace of laughter in my ear, but it may not even be hers) — yet I can see the noonday promenade at the spa, a large number of people, I cannot say whether I was following her or just how I tried to catch her attention — only this much is certain, my boundless emotions had been discovered, and the following occurs: I am seized from behind, below my shoulders, by both arms, and before I know what is happening, I am pushed through the crowd and deposited in the bright sunlight before Fräulein Hueber, who is thus prevented from continuing her walk. And now, while the two hands relentlessly tighten their viselike grip, a cheerful voice above my head relates to her, accurately, I believe, my secret story. I don't understand how I could ever make further use of all the blood that turned to shame in my face. I hope I lost it in a great nosebleed. But now I think of the man and why he did that. Perhaps he loved her? —

My God, but if I should tell you now, my confidante, where I sought refuge, again and again, from such shocks, what every-day life was like compared to those exceptional moments, it seems to me that, strictly speaking, there was no love in it. Not that we didn't affect or have endearing names for each other, or, when we said good night, rather thoroughly undergo separation and hope for another meeting — all this was present (I almost think: too much so), but it did not flow unconditionally from a source of inner wealth and generosity. We might even have saved ourselves the trouble if a certain mistrust of life had not constantly exacted it of us. Just as certain dogs will not eat unless someone pretends to be taking the food from their bowl, we reached for each other only because there were illnesses and unpredictable dangers, because there was always someone dying and because one could become so strangely separate over all this. What held us together must have been, above all, some kind of fear, yes, that's what it was, we were all afraid of—and for—one another, a timorous fear of life and death which we exhaled and, diluted with only a tiny amount of real air, sucked back into our lungs. Besides, it was clear that a quite unknown future lay before me, and an effort was made to gain control over that future while it was still very small, so that it would grow up in captivity, as it were, and never experience its own wildness. When I think of my father, I am almost sure now that he was unable to love; to the end of his life, he had a kind of inexpressible heart-fear of me, a feeling before which I was virtually defenseless and that may have cost him more than the mightiest love, for while it demanded of him the same motions, it never granted him the repose which a lover (I assume) finds in his love, in its ample spiritual certainties.

You you (how shall I address you unprematurely, yet affectionately enough for my heart that streams toward you?) — Look: I am reliving all this for the first time. You are making it real for me, almost out of nothing (for what did I know of this?). I have to write very slowly, the words come like the first heavy drops from the winepress of my memory. I sense that somewhere in that fabled past is where I will have to begin with my love for you — beginner that I am.

Friday, February 13, early

The postcard from Berlin: how glad I am it is here, everything seemed so distant to me, so silent. I am ignorant of geography, which doesn't trouble me greatly, but I have no idea: Are you farther away now, or more accessible? No matter, you are inconceivably close, in any event. So I'll just quickly send off all these pages, the femme de ménage is already here. My God, the amount of reading you'll have to do. — I think it should be Sunday where you are. Oh love.

R.

Benvenuta to Rilke

Written on the tenth while traveling

Dearest — I have thought a lot about your last letter and believe I may be able to clarify something for you. You ask why you always had that gesture of "taking back"? Perhaps because you were mostly surrounded by people who had too little "Nature" to offer your innermost being, your devotion, who expected gratitude from you for their understanding (which never went beyond a feeble wish to understand), or a word in response to their silence; *claiming* all this instead of just being, like the sun or a blooming tree, like a landscape

45

that lets people grow without asking "What will you give me in return?" Perhaps you have never known anyone who became rich in the blessedness of "just being," who had found in it what he needed for his fulfillment, because he himself was the promise and the fulfillment of his own existence. Don't you think that before such a person, once one had recognized him, doubt would have to yield; that perhaps it would recur occasionally, like the last admonition of a long illness that is growing more and more drowsy and dreamlike in the warmth of convalescence—until it is forgotten? And if you never expected anything like this: Isn't it possible to wait for the one before whom doubts lose their bearing and certainties gather in strength, to prepare ever more readily and confidently for his reception? But perhaps he would come quite unexpectedly—the way the voices of a thousand birds will awake overnight and chant spring and sunrise through the window of one who has spent the long winter brooding in his room. Perhaps he would come after long travail and crucifixion, resurrected in his Lord, fearless, full of deep, radiant confidence! — I don't ask whether I have frightened you with ideas and images that are perhaps too audacious for one who dares to put them in words. I don't ask because I bestow upon you all the nameless trust, because it lies in your hands, fearless as a child that does not want to know your intentions, for it is content to be under this dear protection, and (its most human trait) glad to be allowed to partake of your gentle, wakeful, gradually brightening confidence, which it sees coming. — For this shall be the blessing of your summer: to have an ever more conscious connection of your own with humanity. I believe that the longing to be like a saint has strangely misled you away from your own nature, from its maturation, from the fruit of your existence, whose blossom you do not yet really know, though you feel the need for it, perhaps far more than you imagine. But your art, ". . . born into what is human," is meant to be the work of a human being with all his weaknesses and splendors, and not wander off into some remote extra-human heights. I believe your art, in its ultimate perfection, is that of a true human being, though one who carries his God in his heart, who never forgets that he is a friend of the earth, responsive to her life and pulse-beat, penetrating into her ultimate delights as well as into her torments and lowest depths. Is the saint still capable of that? Has the transcendence of everything earthly not robbed him of the vision that is needed for this? For you must consider: The saint is not God; how could he be, since only God's nature in its omnipotence can unite divine and human qualities in itself. But a human being with a God in his heart—must he, *can* he not bear everything, carry all things within himself, live everything for which he is destined? I dare to believe that when you have made this certainty your own, you will no longer have to bear the torment of that aching "Why?" Then you will take of the abundance and be enriched by it—and you will give from the abundance of *your* liberated nature.

And then the flower can blossom of which your longing dreams. And it will wait for the one most holy seed, that it may itself become fruitful: pure and whole.

M.

Rilke to Benvenuta

February 13, toward evening

You must know that I don't read newspapers, but every day I buy two of them, so as to keep myself occasionally informed about exhibitions and the tireless foreign literary life — another reason being that, if I suddenly stopped buying my two journals, the newspaper woman would find it hard to believe that I had all of a sudden lost all interest in the behavior of our time, and would finally be convinced her "Figaro" was not fresh enough for me and swear I was buying one elsewhere. (I sometimes ask myself if love wrongly lived isn't the reason why even in the most superficial human affairs, simple *stopping* is in such bad repute, as though, by right, it should never occur, anywhere?) As for time—our own time—one ought to keep an eye on it, certainly; now, I may only rarely read up on it, but I do occasionally see it in action and have my own wondering thoughts about it. Yesterday morning, for instance, I saw the following: A man standing on a ladder in my alley, painting a marble pattern onto the wooden panels over a storefront, before everyone's eyes, with the good conscience of his profession, the richest marble with truly abundant and ultimately not even entirely improbable veins in it. This goes on in a cheerful and innocent manner, until a little girl—nine or ten years old, but really thin and small, as they are here at that age—crosses the street (especially for this purpose, as I later recognized), stops underneath the paint job and shouts up, cocking her freshly combed head like a sparrow: Ah que c'est beau! Ah que c'est beau! Now I can only say, there was such staggering irony in that brazen bird voice of hers that the man on the ladder must have felt dizzy. I laughed; but once I had turned the corner, it occurred to me that I was about her age when I admitted the difference between real and imitation marble into the circle of my reflections; whenever we entered a restaurant or a stairway, I never failed to test the dubious wall or nearest available pillar with my hand as soon as I could do so without detection, and if it did not pass the test, I would take great care not to expose its secret, but I believe I silently expressed a kind of condolence, as if it had recently lost someone dear — for how far, in those times, was a little boy from irony.

In yesterday's Figaro I found a leading article entitled De l'amour and signed "foemina," which is tantamount to saying Madame Bulteau. I occasionally read this and that by Madame Bulteau, and that decision has to do with the fact that Mme. B. was the best friend of the deceased Countess de la Beaume and that this Mme. de la Beaume left behind two quite remarkable and very impressively crafted books (the second of which surprised even those who had been close to this uncommon and modest woman). It is for the sake of the beautiful books by this other woman that I occasionally read Madame Bulteau, who, incidentally, is quite respectable. (Do you notice how with me everything comes about slyly and furtively — aren't you feeling a bit uneasy?). So I began reading De l'amour too, but did not get very far, yesterday. The thing they call by that name here (and cannot mention often enough), what a curious mixture of virtuosity and incapacity it is; on the one hand as brilliantly done as can be, on the other, it never gets done at all. Do you know what I felt like? — like turning to Plato's Symposium again after a long time. When I first read it, I was living alone in Rome, in a very small house deeply hidden in an old park (the same house where, without knowing what would become of it, I began Brigge).[13] My friend, how well I understood one thing then, how readily inclined I was to realize it, that Eros is not *beautiful;* when Socrates said so and in his temporizing way allowed his younger and more volatile antagonist-interlocutor to explore and gradually block all other paths himself, until in the end only that *one* path was left: that Eros is not beautiful, and Socrates himself took that path toward his god in so pure and serene a spirit — how that set my innermost nature on fire, that Eros cannot be beautiful. I saw him as Socrates invoked him, hard and lean and always a little out of breath, sleepless, worried day and night about the two between whom he walked, to and fro, back and forth, ceaselessly summoned by both: Yes, that was Eros. Truly, how they misjudged him who thought he was beautiful and led a soft life. Ah, slender and tanned and covered with the dust of the road, he never came to rest between the two (for when, I ask, is there not some distance left between them?); and when he arrived, he would speak with great fervor of the other's beauty, inciting each one's heart to become more beautiful, goading it on. Surely there is much in the book — we don't grasp it yet; there was a time when it was grasped — who lost it? How do we spend the millennia? Who among us has the right to speak of *love?*

Behold, Nature does not speak of it; Nature has love in her heart, and no one knows the heart of Nature. Behold, God does not speak of it; God's love is in the world, and the world overwhelms us. Behold, the mother does not speak of it; for her love is in the child, and the child destroys it. Behold, the spirit does not speak of it; for the spirit's love is in the future, and the future is far. Behold, the lover does not speak of it; for the lover's love is in suffering, and suffering weeps. Hush, hush — oh, it is music, then, that would speak. But when music speaks, it does not speak to us. The perfect work of art touches on our condition only in that it outlives us. The poem enters into language from within, from a side that is always averted from us, it fills language wonderfully, it rises within it up to the brim—but it no longer strives to reach us. Colors take shape in a picture, but they are worked into it like rain into the countryside; and the sculptor only shows his stone how to keep its magnificent silence. Music is closer to us, then; it streams toward us; we stand in its way, but then it goes right through us. It is almost like a higher air, we draw it into the lungs of the spirit and it gives us a greater blood in the secret circulation. But how *much* of it surges past us! How *much* of it is borne right through us and we do not grasp it! Alas, we do not grasp it, alas, we lose it.

On an evening, a few days ago, I opened a volume to a plate of El Greco's "Crucifixion," and tried to decipher, in the catalogue of the Prado next to it, what I had written in pencil when I stood before that picture, more seeing than writing. Then I read the word "music."

Behold: before the dark broken heavens the cross with the long pallid flame of his body, and on top, above him, the elaborate inscription, longer than is usual, as though it were the endless name of his sufferings. Mary and John, right and left in the picture, repeating in the turn of their stances the direction of his pain forever held aloft, incapable of doing more than that — only Magdalen, seeing the blood streaming from the crossed and nailed feet, is overcome by the zeal of suffering. She falls to her knees, halts the flow of blood with one hand gripping the stem immediately below the feet and with the other, left, hand far below on the wood: she wants to be the first and the last to catch it—but she is not sufficient. And as she gazes up, helpless, through the black flames of the air—she sees the blood leaping from the wound in his breast and gushing from the marks in his hands: She sees nothing but his blood. But already an angel comes in obliquely, rushing to her side, and helps her — and two angels emerge, moth-pale, beneath the dripping hands in the night space above, and sail toward the blood as if to embrace it, fervently drawn to it with their bare hands, catching it like music.

This sentence here was the one I deciphered first among the smudged lines I had written a year ago— and as I read it now (read it, read it, say it:) is not music in truth like this blood — Magda, have you not sometimes wanted to halt its flowing with your most anguished heart, and could not? Could not have done it without the angels that came to your aid?

The fourteenth, toward dawn

My friend, your letter, the big one, has been here since this morning, but it came together with a lot of correspondence and rushed obligations. I did not want it to be mixed in with all that, nor your picture either; both have been lying there as though tonight, when it grew dark, it would be Christmas Eve. — Benvenuta, now Christmas has come — I have read your pages, I'm going to re-read them in a moment, just as, having been called out of the room where the presents are laid out, one quickly runs back in to take everything in one's hands again. Oh, there they stand, these heavy, heavy presents, in the radiance of my, your — in the celebration of your holy joy. You are so near to me that I cannot write to you for nearness, you are in the air of this room, and only sometimes, bending over your picture, I compare your invisible presence with the soaring wings of your eyebrows in the grave sky of your face.

Rainer

(Tell me a lot about your present good surroundings — a lot about *everything*.)

Benvenuta to Rilke

Berlin
February 11, 1914

Dear heart,

Arrived here yesterday evening late and dead tired; after a long ugly trip. Nothing but an impression of soot, overheated air, bad perfume, crumpled-up pages of some humor magazine, and orange peels; in between, a few faces above well-tailored clothes.

On the table in my room here lay three letters: one good, one indifferent, the third horrible, unmentionable. It brought up the most bitter feelings. . . . Then came a very deep dreamless sleep, and finally morning with the sun shining through the wide window. In the bathroom next door, two swift little feet were trying to keep from pattering, but secretly hoping to be heard nevertheless. When I called out: Betti, why don't you come in, the door was immediately thrown open and a little girl with a long dark braid and wearing a red slip came running in like the fresh morning wind in person, gave my sleepy self one kiss after another, and cried again and again, with touching joy, Aunt Magda, my sweetheart, you're back, you're back! Then the dear little thing scampered off in a hurry for breakfast and school, though not without the most binding assurances of meeting again in four or five hours. There are three children in the house now: Betti, Theo, and Hermann, twelve, fifteen, and nineteen years old. There has to be great fairness in the way the hours are apportioned, so that everyone gets his share. Betti knows that the hour from six to seven in the evening is incontestably hers for reading out loud or for doll's business. The hours after dinner, when the piano in the music room is opened up, are shared between the boys and the "grown-ups"—father and mother Delbruck and Wolfgang, who comes to visit his uncle's house in the evening. This house, a regular, sturdy sort of home, is full of light and strength and cheerful labor; there is in it a radiance of infinite love, the epitome of "mother," which so few people know.

You wanted a picture of everything that surrounds my life here and I have tried to begin by describing it to you. Now there's also my room. The nicest thing about it is a very large window; it faces the garden, there is a lawn, a swing, even a pigeon coop and a useless merry little pinwheel that always incites the two dogs to take up the chase, barking wildly, even though they have known it for years. . . . . .

My dear, dear friend, your picture stands here, the one on a bench outside. I believe that of the three this is the one I am closest to. The picture of me you may perhaps not even care for very much, for it is just one of those new "beautiful" photographs—but a little of me is in it nevertheless, it looks out at you, I think, and my sending it to you is basically egotistical; I shall gaze at it for a long time and imagine it is I and that I can nod at you if your gaze should come to rest on it while you are writing to me.

Let me tell you about the silliest and merriest of all dogs! Right now they are dancing around the little pinwheel as if possessed (I can see it from my desk), and the old major next door is angry—he's threatening them. Poor old man. All he can do, I believe, is scold and threaten them with his cane. Three times the dogs have been to court on his account, and won, of course, so Betti told me. Now the sun beckons me to go outside. I want to go to the post office, to mail a card to you, then walk to Paulsborn and come home at noon with a real appetite for roast veal and rice. In the evening by the lamp I shall find you again—and continue my account.

My dear friend, the penciled pages of the 10th were written during my trip when the train stopped for half an hour in Dresden . . . . now your letter of Sunday,* which I received early this morning, has overtaken them; but you shall have them anyway, since they are yours. How your joy becomes a godsend to me, how you make my heart resound with a thousandfold echo, even when you ask anxious questions, how much of your experience has been mine, and still is—how much, especially of what is hardest for you! — And how my faith in the divine returns to me consciously and visibly—through you. It was always there, you know, it just never acquired a form in consciousness. As a very very young girl I was robbed of it. There was someone who robbed me of my faith, someone who wanted to be God for me himself. Someone who wanted to force his hard, masterful love on my first awakening youth, in order to rule, no, to enslave me. This is a bitter hard story, and its conclusion was that, at the moment when my youthful folly believed that he who had taken God away from me could restore in his own person all that I had lost, he turned away, laughing, and carried off the victory of his god-theft in loveless hands. What is the phrase in the Stories of God?: "God almost died then . . ." — Much bitterness followed, but joy did not die, since joy carries an eternal life within itself. Some day, if you want to hear it, I may tell you everything; then I will hold your hand, and then perhaps I will be allowed to find the flooding relief of infinite tears that are still unshed and that press like a tempestuous stream to join the river of my joyousness and vitality, to be released in it for ever . . . .

I played Bach this evening. Everything became clear again in this divine purity. Some day you shall hear Bach and completely grasp him, so I hope, for I believe that only by passing through many tests of suffering can one arrive at Bach and his infinity.

In the afternoon, as I was writing, Betti knocked and asked a favor of me: a friend of hers was visiting, and she would so much like to — — in short, I shut away my letter sheets and went with her to the music room. Then the two little girls sat hand in hand on the sofa, and the one translucent sonata by the young Mozart turned into a second one — and then we sang a few of Reinecke's dear songs for children. Storytelling, also, was given its due; they already knew so very much about little Mozart from an old book, and then I told them, as well as I could, about the "Journey to Prague."

Dearest, it is late — there is so very very much to talk about — and ultimately, what can words on a piece of paper really express! One more thing: when people don't know what it's all about, why don't you just let them feel some rays of the great warmth, those rays that pass through them toward distant goals. For you are so rich in the fullness of your heart, my brother, and have inexhaustible wellsprings of soul. This is why all the things you doubt will resolve themselves. *How* I believe in this!

Magda

Berlin
February 14, 1914

Dearest — what a good, long beautiful letter that was! It has turned all my resolutions to naught, for I was going to leave off writing to you for four, five days, so that your work sheets won't get jealous. Did I have a premonition? Today you write that one of them was slightly reproachful, now comes the letter you began on the ninth and finished yesterday — and I read it and was already at my desk to send you a visible greeting. Do you know what I would like to do? I want to make your heart shine as it never dreamed it could! As if it had never known the meaning of *light* and all the other concepts that adorn and surround it! —

Yesterday friends of the family came to visit, many people, and I played, but they were so touchingly ignorant, and had no idea that all the warmth and depth of Beethoven's Sonata in E Major was flying past them (or through them) to you, to your lonely moonlit window; some of them had tears in their eyes, and a very young girl kissed me spontaneously, the way children do when they wrap their arms around your neck. But this morning, when I arrived late at the breakfast table, I found a

56

wreath of yellow tulips surrounding the prosaic rolls. They were worlds apart from the gleaming pot that stood singing on the little gas flame, and yet all who were present were in splendid spirits. A freshly boiled egg, two small silver knives, and the butter tray, which was trying very hard to look "sophisticated." There I sat alone (for the others had left to pursue the day and its obligations), taking pleasure in Aunt Berta's pretty gift, the tulips, and my head was filled with a hundred solutions of musical problems and a great eagerness to get to work, and something else, a quiet expectation of eleven o'clock (that's when the second mail arrives); the first had only brought a letter from my Berlin agent, as well as an offer, which sounds quite attractive, to play in Warsaw next fall. Then a piano tuner came and I had to take refuge in theory. Just as I had become engrossed in Breithaupt's wonderful book, happy to discover how much of what he expresses I had already unconsciously found out, Jeschke arrives like fate itself, inexorable but benign (he's the servant here, a most original character about whom one could write a book), bearing upon a small wooden tray a truly enormous letter with its attendant registration slip. Are there words to express how wonderful it feels to receive such a letter? There are none, but you already know it.

And now I write to you with a thousand thoughts and a pen that is much too slow. Do you know what we'll do? I have to go to Zurich around March 15 to discuss musical matters with Volkmar Andrae — it may take five days or so; and then you will say a little word, and perhaps in Geneva we could—? What do you think? My yellow monster tells me that Geneva can be reached in eight hours by express train from Paris and from Zurich in six. Or we could choose another place, not too far, for I have to keep a strict budget and frequently consult a black purse containing blue bills. But what does it matter if it's empty some day — one just starts working again and everything will be as it should be. Why don't you write me today whether you want to do that — and especially whether the sheets on your desk go along with it — for one should not experience something so beautiful without their blessing —

Yesterday evening I had already gone to bed, I read (after who knows how many times before) "Maria's Death," and again and again, when it says "But the angels took her unto themselves . . . ," such a deep emotion comes over me, I could never describe it. No, dear, don't try, you won't persuade me of your prejudice against yourself—though I believe in what you call bad and crude, even brutal in yourself, I believe that *you could* . . . (so you say), but it does not frighten me, for I know that you require only those few things you need for the sake of the deepest task—the right proportion, "the Good," as you call it. Once you have that, you will be saved; all of this is so simple and clear, my dear, my good friend; listen into it, you will see, suddenly you will have that great confidence, and it will never leave you again. If I may, I will help you to find it, I won't turn against you, how could I, since I see your heart? And if I may ask you to bring it to me, especially in its greatest uncertainty, in the anguish of its doubts, I ask also that you let me love and protect it, and tell it that I know what it is: Neither a bright, rigid spot in the rock, nor something dull and heavy; it's just a human heart — and tell it also what it means to *me:* a home with wide-open doors where one is neither shut in nor asked to leave; doors that are simply there, always open and ready; a home of a kind so rarely known to man that there is an amazement about it and a jubilation within.

Haven't we known each other before, on another star? In Heaven? Before we came to earth as human beings?

M.

Rilke to Benvenuta

My sister, what purities, what luminosities, what storms of feeling toward you in my soul. For that's what it is, in you my thoughts attain their purity and no impure thought can exist, because it could not exist in you. That life in the spirit for which I have been struggling all these unspeakable years (do you understand, in the spirit, a spirit of such immensity that it can sweep everything along in its course, excluding nothing), that infinite life in the spirit, in you it comes true for me, I gaze into it as into the most innocent landscape.

. 14

Precious sister, your joyousness, your confidence in me, your suffering—: I don't know which of these feels closest to me, or most pure, most intelligible to my heart, as if it were my own feeling and I had only to hold still beneath it, — it touches me everywhere, as the inside of my lids touches my eyes.

— — I take leave of you, dearest, just like little Betti, with the understanding, as absolute and urgent as can be, that I will find you again in four or five hours; I am going to write a letter, perhaps a very long one, concerning Duse,[15] for which I am qualified by nothing whatsoever except my soul's restless desire to keep a theater open for her somewhere in the most unlikely possibility that she will suddenly be able to act again. I can't imagine her sinking away into illness or into some wayward, murky obscurity. I feel that she should go down in a

glorious setting, in the same place where she rose so magnificently: on the stage. I can't forget it, I went through it two years
ago: she wanted to act, one more time, bien armée mais tran-
quille, as she told me, — just imagine: The moment passed
(and all it *could* be is a moment, consumed as she is), it passed
because no one seized it, because nothing was ready, because
the few people who could have made it possible discussed
various courses of action instead of *taking* action. Dearest, it
felt to me as if the dying Chopin were yearning to play once
more, to play so as to lead his soul into the eternal world —
and all the people around him were talking about *whether* a
piano was available and *whether* one should have it brought
upstairs and how expensive that might be. There was a summer in Venice (I am there often, with one of those families, an
old Venetian one, where I am occasionally permitted for a
little while to be a child of the house) — I was living in a very
beautiful little apartment filled with things from the Ottocento,
each one full of feeling, a charming clavecin stood there, no
one played it — the apartment is a small, permanent pied-à-
terre belonging to some dear friends, I did not pay them, used
all my money for roses, always had plenty of them, in silver
bowls, I tended them like a cool fire that flares up in the
senses, never letting them go out. When no one else had roses
any longer (and they become rare in the Venetian summers),
they stayed with me, as if they couldn't let go. — Dear heart, at
that time Duse came to visit me often — she lived very near
by, suddenly her gondola would turn from the lagoon into my
canal, I could recognize her from my desk. For years and years
I had longed for a meeting with her, without ever wanting to
make the slightest effort to bring it about, and imagine, now
God, in his unimplorable grace, had showered me with a
thousand blessings, granting me not just *one* meeting, but
many, daily ones—at her home, at mine, with Venice for a

background, — it sounds like a fairy tale, and undeserving, as in a fairy tale, one lived deep within it—lived? Suffered, suffered, oh Benvenuta, for it was this that hammered a rift through my whole inner nature, that what for a few years had been a gloriously unstinting, princely fulfillment, now became no more than the velvet pillow that supports the head of the "dying Gaul" in the Museo degli Thermi in Rome—: a soft, beautiful bedding for a still unknown irrevocable suffering. At any rate, we saw each other often, I'm not sure why, perhaps out of an urge to help one another — but there was so much misfortune in each of us — when we heaped it all up, we would finally stand on top, as though on a pyre that towered day and night in a pure but lifeless air, and though we never told each other, neither of us could imagine a future, except perhaps one in which God would set the final flame to this parched foundation that would consume it and us together. —

Two hours later: Sister, it's done; like a storm I descended upon that poor person to whom I wrote it, who will read it amid thunder and lightning, for these entered into my eight pages — I can't go on now — Until later.

Later

The "events," dear child, and what part of them still encroaches upon you — I know that one cannot speak of this, except at that hour (which will come) that is gently set apart from all events; so I will just quietly take them in — heavy as they are, they sink into my blood, to join so many things that are beyond comprehension and beyond relief . . . Five years, that was the length of my military education, from my tenth to my fifteenth year (what years!) — I think this is the utmost limit, no one has ever stayed under water longer. At times, since then, I have come to understand the legend that is gradually growing out of that far-off, defenseless suffering; sometimes it is too much for me even now; for I went through it at a time of my life when it impressed itself on every part of the still pliable future. Nevertheless, whenever a fragment, already transformed into legend, does reach my consciousness, I marvel at the glory of the suffering endured, I stand as though before colossal burial mounds and cannot measure up to the might and valor it has acquired in death.

But now let me just add this: Magda. If you should feel some day (and since yesterday there have been times when such a feeling has quietly risen in me and dissolved again) — if you feel that our timeless hour should be *soon,* if you crave it like sleep or a drink of water — if you think it might enable you to absolve a still impending past with greater serenity, as though it had already gently arrived — if you should feel all this even for an instant: Then, dear, dear heart, let us look calmly and thoughtfully ahead and arrange the days, wherever, whenever, however you wish, as many as you want, as soon as it seems right to you. Promise me that. As you know, I am fairly free. What holds me here is my conscience concerning my work, my dutiful submission to this stubborn regularity, to which I myself have pledged and bound myself, knowing very well why; as things stand now, you would not interrupt it from without, but from within: and of that I must not be afraid. — So much for that. On the other hand, you can see how I am living, living in you, attempting a new life of the spirit in the wonderful fact of your having come to me, sheltered in you already. If there is a closeness apart from what is obviously visible, then this pure aspiration of my heart toward you, this flood of my being, this reverence of my nature must be an almost unsurpassable closeness, and you, Magda, cannot help but feel it.

Yesterday I lay awake for some time, thinking about the sorrows of your childhood. My feeling circled it from afar, like a lion circling a fire in the desert at night—; sister, as the profoundly Slavic man that I am in some part of my nature, I almost envied you for this violence that was done to you. When one considers how it drew you into yourself, made you into a creature—which would not have been so readily possible in the face of a vaguely distant God—how day after day it made you wrestle and converse with otherwise barely conceivable powers: One's heart leaps at the thought of the splendor that some day must issue for you from this deceit of an arrogant man. It occurred to me how in the Russian soul, which recognizes no boundary between divine and human harshness, this experience might have revealed itself more immediately, directly, as what it essentially was: a fall of God in an experience of God.

If you knew what dogs mean to me when I watch them (it would be wrong for me to own one), you would not doubt that I *saw* them as you showed them to me from your window, those two "silliest and merriest" of all dogs. They and the little pinwheel and the major; to my mind this group resembles those three magnificently simple-minded marionettes, Kasper, Princess, and Owl, which I bought last fall in Munich with Ruth, in an old stationery shop behind Papa Schmidt's puppet theater, in order that someone, that is, Regine Uhlmann (of whom I will tell you some day), might write a real play for them — I, of course, can't think of anything — just for these three, who are so far apart from each other that there is space enough for the liveliest action. (I wonder whether Betti, and you with her, could make up some nice complications involving the three of them and, mind you, a proper *development* also, something that would come about if one were to leave them to their own devices on the stage of a beautiful marionette theater representing, say, a terrible prison.) (Or?)

Dear, I write "Ruth," and you, timelessly familiar friend, you don't even know yet that I have a small daughter (small? twelve years old, like Betti), a schoolgirl of resolute, womanly temper, carefree, quite solid and practical — whom I see rarely, but with whom I maintain a good and slightly mischievous friendship, just as I have become a more and more reliable distant-close friend to her mother — at least I hope so — after all that has happened. They live together in Munich; Clara Rilke[16] is a highly gifted sculptor, a student of Rodin, coming from Bremen.

. . . 17

We meet as friends whenever I come to Munich — Ruth has a natural, unbroken relationship to her mother as well as to me; since I was always away, these relationships were bound to develop quite separately anyway. — That I cannot be of much use to children, given my uncertainties and worries about myself — (all their asking and tugging and testing truly requires the most extraordinary equanimity and cheerful serenity, indeed some kind of finality, in the adult) — this you will understand; but some aspects of my relationship to Ruth, which I myself only half know and cannot explore very deeply in my feelings, will gradually present and express themselves in relation to you, and I foresee that you will make much of it fruitful for me. — The reason why I haven't written to you about this whole world until now is that it has been standing ever more separate next to mine, in fact not even next to it, but somewhere in its own place — so that actually it does not belong in the same constellation with the solitary rising and setting of my heart, and where its effects reach in to my world nonetheless, it treats me with a kind of gentle indulgence, if I'm not mistaken, with an increasingly reproachless patience and a clarified warmth of wishing that I might find and act

64

upon what is mine and do it justice: For after all, no one can repair whatever wrong he may have done, except within himself.

Imagine, a visitor came, my door leads directly into the stairwell, the moment I open it I'm already lost — a painter who wanted information about a new publishing house, a new magazine (my God, the things they publish nowadays, and what they look like); in short, we agreed that the times are taking curious paths in the world of art, that we had learned things differently; he aged visibly as we talked, our apprenticeships receded, crowded out by so much novelty, into time immemorial. Not I, I did not grow old, my apprenticeship is not over yet. When he had become so old that he could just barely walk, I quickly gave him the Proust as a present, so that he would leave — not mine, that one is for you, it will be mailed tomorrow morning, together with this letter. Good night.

Yes, about Proust there is one more thing I must tell you, the pencil marks are really just footprints I left as I went through the book, showing where I stood still, surprised, pensive, pleased, or simply attentive; and firmer lines where I enjoyed walking back and forth several times. They mean no more than that. Furthermore, I find the second part, despite some good ideas and many little discoveries, almost boring, often no more than a "roman" of the kind the French cannot cease to produce, now from the right, now from the left. Only the passages near the end about the phrase in the sonata and the music struck here and there, at unrelated intervals, on the countless keys of the universe — these passages alone are, possibly, among the most important parts within the many, it's fair to say, overcrowded pages. Also some more passages in the third part. — I just noticed that I wrote a comment in the front[18] which, as it stands, is thoroughly biased: Also, I remember it was supposed to bring out the book's basic flaw as against its hundred merits, which extend, in tones and half-tones, by way of inexhaustible variations, from the merely amusing to the truly significant — virtues that I recognized immediately and with such certainty that I did not feel the need to make any note of them.

But how will you manage not to let this fat book take you away from either the children or the grown-ups? I don't want that on my conscience, and besides, the little pinwheel also wants to be looked at occasionally from your desk — and I, what will become of me, once you begin reading?

Rainer

The morning of the sixteenth

Now look, this proves I have no talent after all: Here I've been living (for thirty-eight years) beneath this sky, and when I wake up, as I did today, at the break of dawn and the moon stands in the middle of my southern window (she looked rather unwell and neglected, by the way, and left immediately, high as she stood, to hide in the gloom), I am perfectly certain she must have made a mistake, that's how out of place she looks to me *there* — I said to her, "But my dear—" and gone she was, not, I imagine, with an entirely good conscience, and yet of course she was right. — Then I think of the seventeen-year-old Tycho Brahe, how he left his noble Danish clan to study law in Leipzig, actually dabbling in it a little, but at night (and Leipzig nights are not exactly of prime quality) leaning out of his small window when his tutor was asleep and silently impressing the constellations into a sphere that was no bigger than his fist and could be comfortably concealed, thus ena-bling his vision to receive the night sky as if by dictation in the purest order—I'm almost tempted to say, in sequence—his soul sang it at sight, straight from the score (dearest, that is genius); you see, and a year later, on the estate of his uncle Bille, walking home slowly in the evening, he saw with his bare eyes the new star in the Cassiopeia; so familiar was he with this numberless vault that the small, silent addition became simply visible to him, as a teacher will notice a shy newcomer standing among the other boys in his class.

And I — I just wonder about the moon in a dull sort of way, suspecting it of carelessness in its heavenly behavior — thus the world favors us, each of us, in unequal measure. Not that I want to figure or wangle or spy it out, no — just to go more and more deeply into the law for the contemplation and joy of it — for there one treads lightly and does not grow tired.

(Dearest, do you like the name Rainer? I was christened René Maria . . . and a few more names following those — if it's easier for you to call me René — do as you feel; when I was a child, René felt closer to me, later it was Rainer, which became more and more authentic and valid along with my books.) Farewell, otherwise the femme de ménage will interrupt me, she'll be here any moment, if I could only just go on writing everything to you, dearest. Every time I stop, I feel like the woman who came out of church and thought she had prayed all she could — when she reached the next corner, she turned around and had to go back and sink to her knees.

Your affectionate friend

Benvenuta to Rilke

Sunday the fifteenth. Morning.

When I read your childhood and all that is fearful, joyous, unconscious, and blessed as it appears in your memory, it makes me wonder whether the very first sensations, which one only recalls as if in a dream, don't have a decisive influence on the rest of one's life. I always feel that we keep our childhood locked inside, in a hidden cabinet, for he was really right, St. Augustine was: where should it have gone? We carry it with us, and we see it most clearly in those moments when we are able to feel passionately responsive to children. Some people, I think, have buried their childhood, or they have done something terrible: They have murdered it. These are the sad characters one sees passing by an innocent face and open little arms with indifference; or else with a bad conscience.

Imagine, my first memory reaches way down into the deepest unconscious: there was a piano made of some light-colored wood; I was sitting near it in a little high chair, my mother was singing, and I began to cry. Later she often sang the same song, and it always brought me to this feeling of painful compassion. Years later, I became conscious of the words, and learned them by heart. Here they are:

> Ich habe dich überall gesucht
> in Wald und Flur und Hain.
> Ich fand dich nicht,
> du musst mir wohl
> zu tief im Herzen sein.*

The second, already much brighter memory is of a birthday: three years old. On the table stood the fulfillment of my most ardent longing: a small "Einspänner," as they call it in Vienna, a one-horse carriage, painted a patriotic black and yellow, a shiny brown horse hitched to the front — in addition, there

---

* I have sought you everywhere/ in wood and grove and field./ I found you not./ You must be deep/ inside my heart concealed. [Tr.]

were two tiny dolls, who were immediately christened Josef and Minna. Then there is a gap; with my sixth year came an event, the visit of a cousin from South America, and when I was seven, something marvelous: the first piano lesson. For a long time I stood at the window, waiting to get a glimpse of "her," who was going to make something utterly incomprehensible real for me, but of course she came from the opposite side and was suddenly standing in the room; still quite a young girl in a purple dress (oh this velvet dress!), and then the notes were explained. The lines connecting the sixteenth notes looked to me like the long chimneys of steamships (every day lots of steamships passed our house on the Danube), chimneys that bend down as they approach a bridge and rise up again after passing it. Already a year later I gave my first performance at a little student recital, playing a Mozart sonata "by heart" and a few little pieces by Grieg. . . . . . And do you know who was among the listeners? Fräulein Hueber! This is not a joke. If she was rather tall and blond and named Olga, she must have been the one from the Bohemian spa! I still know her and visit her now and then. She is much older than I, has changed her name in the meantime, for she got married—no longer young—eight or ten years ago.

Now I must leave again and don't feel like saying farewell at all, for there is no leave-taking between us. My dear dear heart! Give me your hand and imagine my telling you everything that could make your eyes bright and your heart glad.

Magda

Late in the evening

I dreamed at dusk that I was sitting at the piano—and suddenly a special brilliance entered the sounds, as never before. And as I, amazed, gave myself over to this unknown feeling, I felt that you had come. Was it necessary to turn around to the door through which you had entered? No, you were there, palpably—and your eyes encompassed brilliance and dusk, all resonance and joy in their gaze. But I was filled only with a profound, desireless bliss, content to rest in that gaze of yours. With this the day ends. Did you feel it in your lonely room by the green-shaded lamp? Your little picture stands before me. Good night!

The sixteenth. Afternoon

. . . Rainer, how deeply, deeply moved I am—by the Christmas of your silent evening. Brother, closest friend, am I that important to you? That much more essential than anything else that you could make a *Christmas* out of a few pages and a picture—of *me?* Do you realize what you are giving me? For the first time in my life a gift, truly a heavenly gift, that is *not* binding. Everything I have received from people until now (despite my deep affection for a few of them) always had a background of having to say thank you, and however gladly those thanks were given and taken, there was always a sense of responsibility: whether I had clothed my gratitude in sufficiently emphatic and convincing words.

But now *you* are there—and I thank you as I would the spring sky, or a branch of golden fruits, or the radiance of a wide surface of water in the morning, or the beauty of brilliant snow-covered mountain peaks in the glow of evening.

Dear Rainer—you have made me very happy!

M.

February 17, 1914

Yesterday I heard Ferruccio play again, after not having heard him for a long time . . . . . with the Hammerklavier Sonata the revelation, *his* revelation, was complete, especially

70

in that ineffable, nameless something, which—since one has to "call" it by a name—is known as the "third movement." And the face of the forty-seven-year-old, so strangely and suddenly aged, who sat there, truly bringing the sounds from heaven down to earth, this face became young and happy in his contemplation of Beethoven, released, freed from all the gravity of life. And then I experienced something remarkable. Behind me sat Ossip Shubin, whom I know—and next to her an old lady. The latter managed to rattle some little balls (bonbons, perhaps) in a manner that made one's blood race. Ossip must have heard it too, but made no move to stop it. I finally turned around, I'm sure with an exasperated, disturbed, burning glance—torn away from my contemplation of Beethoven's heaven—and probably also said something very softly. At the end she tapped me on the shoulder, and when I turned around, she modestly told me her name and said more or less the following: I thank you for the good lesson, your eyes gave me a real fright, for it was only your look that made me conscious of my enormous thoughtlessness. —

That was beautiful, wasn't it? I became very fond of that old lady. Then the intermission was over and there came the light drifting clouds and the soft flight of butterflies as in a breath of yellow roses: Chopin. And what this blessedly gifted mind, what his blessed hands made of that! Marvels upon marvels! Sometimes it seems almost unbearable, almost too much for a human heart.

I still have a lot to tell you about this, as you must tell me more about Duse—and Venice. Oh, roses! I have always had the greatest longing to see roses in silver bowls (not to own them, my desire never ventured that far), an abundance, an abundance. You know, in Florence there are roses such as I've never seen, with that strange intimate red and a completely different scent than elsewhere. Also the familiar light La

France—and the snow queens—and the "Sultan of Zanzibar," black-red, with an intoxicating scent. I once had a garden in Hietzing (we lived in a wonderful little house which Fischer von Erlach had built for the Empress Maria Theresa), and there I planted many little rosebushes. Oh Rainer, that garden! I shall have to tell you about it some time. And how I carried much sadness and heaviness into its roses; the whole of a disillusioned youth! And how its rural stillness and the wealth of its orchard blossoms (for there were many orchard trees) gave me peace—and the courage to long for summer—and for music. Again and again. For this was the only way to endure the wrong of a marriage founded on ignorance and pity—a bond which is now about to be dissolved . . . . . .

Yesterday I told Betti the story of "Tom Thumb." The child looked at me as if I had never told a story before — and then for a long time everything was quiet. Finally Betti said hesitantly (quite unlike her usual manner): I think such stories are almost too beautiful for me—but even so, you have to tell them to me often again.

And then later: you know, I have a very very small pillow — do you think it could perhaps also— —?

So now we are embroidering a "Good Lord" for Mother Delbruck. He (or it!) is the small pillow, and I am sewing tiny flowers with white silk on white batiste. As a reward, she reads me a marvelous fairy tale: Zapfel Kern's adventures, and we laugh a lot about the gay little jumping jack. (Later in the afternoon) You ask me whether I like the name Rainer. Yes, I like it, better than René, but I would most like to call you by a name that is yours and that no one else has called you. It would be like a present, such a name, hardly remembered by anyone and therefore ours alone. Think about it . . . . . . Now the book has arrived too. How touched I was by the purple.ribbon that was wound around it! All this is your closeness, but also the distance of a time when we did not yet know each other. (Was there ever such a time? How could there be?)

Very late evening—actually nighttime

I went out this evening, to a concert in the Lyceum Club, was supposed to meet many people, for the tiresome "necessary" reasons. But some interesting musicians were there: Van Lier, the cellist, Adele aus der Ohe, Sharvenka too. Then I played various things from Liszt's "Années de Pèlerinage." And again it was you who gave me the most beautiful moment among so many unknown charming people. I imagined as I played what it would be like if you stood leaning by that dark picture on the other side of the room — we would look at one another with a loving and secret understanding. Rainer — perhaps in twenty—in eighteen days— —?

Good night. I write to you half in a dream, dearest, precious, sleep well!

M.

Rilke to Benvenuta

Monday, February 16

Precious girl, I continue writing, addressing to your heart this incomprehensible journal of my desire to live·— I feel as if this were my final, definitive work, to make myself true to you, true, do you hear, not likable — adamantly true — as if in your heart I might, for the first time, make myself plain to God, so that he would know me, saying: Here, Lord, see here the metals of my being, they rang against the pavement like the coin that is tossed to a beggar (why shouldn't it be a larger one occasionally?) — but what is needed now is to collect them, to see whether it is possible to fuse them into an alloy and to prepare for the bell which you will perhaps some day want to break out of me, once the mold appears ready to you. Lord, impress upon my feeling that there is a sacred kinship in these unassayable metals, that they will be capable of blending as one into a thing possessed of a soul, a thing that no longer rings against stone, but finds its feelings above in your beautiful air, favoring neither the birds and the angels.

And then, Magda, there enters into this limpid stream of feeling toward you the fear of incapacity (this ever-present fear that by now has sunk such profound roots in me), for I know I am not like the days of the year which arise one from the other; rather, the overabundance of utterable experience can turn at one blow into its most rigid opposite, like that strange river that unexpectedly descends beneath the earth with its living waters — Oh love, when I have this fear, I immediately want to reach out to you in all my boundless breadth, but *cannot,* and am forced to destroy the front ranks of my troops and dispatch them man by man through the narrow gorge of these inhospitable pages — this humiliates my troops and detains them indefinitely, and you cannot receive the right impression of their freedom of movement. These must be the agonies of one who yearns for eternal bliss; he feels that his prayers advance him only bit by bit, while the angels stand there, unimpressed. Ah, if he were to burst so gloriously, in one piece, whole, into the beyond, almost startling the heavens with the reckless ardor of his soul — he would first have to die. This, if I died in you, this is how you would feel me, and you wouldn't even be startled, for to you it would be second nature to encompass me as a whole: you great, you greater circle around the infinite circle of my heart. Like John the

Evangelist in Memling's picture at Bruges — that's how I want to write to you here on the rock-laden island of my heart, swept over by the storm of ecstasy, write to you with this right hand, write to you with this left hand, obeying the ray of speech, and never stop writing to you.

You my true child and my true virgin mother, dear girl: What miracles have befallen us and continue to befall us; sometimes I hold my breath, in the midst of some task, in the street, while falling asleep or waking up at night, hold my breath and listen inward to hear if it really is happening always, always: Yes, it is happening.

The day before yesterday, at the very end, there was something I haven't told you about. Imagine: My most youthful poem, the "lay" of my ancestor, the Cornet Christoph Rilke, who (in 1662?) rode against the Turks, galloped in a *foreign,* rich, chivalrous language through this heart that is now set athunder by you. Suddenly this poem, after having been forgotten for many years, is being translated all over the world. English, Polish, Hungarian — Heaven knows what other translations have been offered to the publisher in recent months. Now an Italian one had arrived, and quite an accomplished one, it seemed to me: I read it twice out loud in the tall silence of the room; it came back to me in the foreign language, for which I feel a great affinity, as if sprung to life in a different blood, I thought of the single wind-blown moon night when I wrote it (—fifteen years ago . . .), and felt as though at that time I had known the shortest path through my heart, or was it a path at all — didn't I race head on over shrubs and fences? — The little youthful portrait of my father must have had an additional effect on me, and probably also a picture of his brother, who had died young, whom I had never known except on that small oil painting that showed him in his slender lancer's uniform shortly before his death (he died, I believe, of pneumonia, contracted by a fall from his horse in some cold rapids). This may have been the original inspiration that helped me take off from those few scanty lines about the Cornet I had culled from archival records and placed before me, using them as a rocket that could be sent with a spark of ardor on its bold, irrepressible curve through the spacious night of my anticipated future. — Back then, when, light-hearted, in a dreamily productive night (for producing a poem did not yet entail such incalculable responsibilities), I learned, guessed, how great a thing it was to race with hot cheeks from the warmth of childhood through a moment of manhood into death—: Sister, I had no notion then how I would later admire those who died young, not for the way they rushed past, but actually for their being dead, for the superiority, the forbearance, the mildness with which they look back at us in death. In every country I have sought them out, their pictures, their letters, their shadowy poems—; and how touchingly generous it seemed to me that they had taken the time to love a girl without being afraid that the cost of expectation (all those hours of waiting in vain when one is in love) might be too great for the brief time they had. When in Rome, quite incomprehensibly, I had my first encounter with the invented figure of Malte, I was shaken by the immediate realization that he would have to die young. And when later, as I was developing Malte's relations, I invented little Erik, who is so highly favored by the spirits, it was this again that I found strangely absorbing: The durations and emptinesses and endless details of childhood that succeeded each other at such a leisurely, even pace, unabbreviated, as though there were all the time in the world, even in a life qui n'aura qu'un tout petit lendemain transparent. In Padua, where one can see the tombstones of many young people who died there (during their studies at the famous university), in Bologna, in Venice, in Rome, every-

76

where I stood, a student of death, before their boundless erudition and let myself be educated.

You too must remember them from Genoa and Verona, how they rest in the churches, youthfully prone figures, without envy of our coming or going, inwardly self-sufficient, as if in the agony of death they had more than ever sunk their teeth into the fruit of life and were now savoring endlessly the depths of its sweetness. (For there is no end.)

The seventeenth (early)

Let me tell you, I am on the tracks of such wondrous things. I love gazing into things. Can you imagine with me how glorious it is, for example, to see into a dog, in passing — *into* him (I don't mean to see through him, which is merely a kind of human gymnastics, where one comes right back out on the other side of the dog, using him as a window to whatever human concerns lie behind him, no, not that) — but to ease oneself into the dog exactly at his center, the place out of which he exists as a dog, that place in him where God would, so to speak, have sat down for a moment when the dog was complete, in order to watch him at his first predicaments and notions and let him know with a nod that he was good, that he lacked nothing, that no better dog could be made. For a while one can endure being in the middle of the dog, but one has to be sure to jump out in time, before the world closes in around him completely, otherwise one would remain the dog within the dog and be lost to everything else. Ah, will you laugh, dear trusted friend? If I were to tell you *where* my greatest feeling, my universal feeling, the bliss of my earthly existence has been, I would have to confess: It has always, here and there, been in this kind of in-seeing, in the indescribably swift, deep, timeless moments of this divine seeing into the heart of things.

77

You see, and when one loved, this was the first thing that fell away — the dog would come along: an inexpressible pain would arise, one no longer had the prodigal freedom to merge with him. There was someone in the background who called you "mine" (that irresponsible word), and the dog would have to introduce himself first to that person and ask permission to let you enter him for one imperceptible, secret moment, exactly the way one asks permission to take a little girl out for a drink of hot chocolate. No dog would think of doing such a thing, and if he did, it would ultimately not be the same, indeed it would not be anything at all. For once someone knew of it and allowed it so and so many times ("just this once more"), that would suffice to make that enchanted moment impossible almost forever.

Dearest, am I utterly foolish and childish to say this? But you have no idea *how seriously* I experienced this; I could imagine that I left home simply for the reason that one was not allowed "to go into the dog," or, if one ever succeeded, one would have to tell what it was like inside the dog. And to be honest with myself, I really cannot imagine anyone, no mother either, who could bear living with a child, if that child happens to be destined to recklessly roam in and out of all sorts of creatures. And I can also put myself sufficiently far in the mother's place to understand that some real harm is being inflicted on her, for to her the dog is scarcely more decent than some tavern by the harbor; how could she comprehend that her clean little boy feels at home in *there* and not in the least with her? What do you think? Or the one left behind would have to be a sort of sailor's bride and not have any notion of the dangers and fates and adventures from which her beloved will perhaps (perhaps!) return some day or in the middle of the night, darkly taciturn, his senses saturated with foreign images, foreign tastes, foreign feelings, incapable for weeks of saying anything about all that, almost as if his blood itself had turned strange and foreign. Oh, is it even imaginable that she, who has been waiting for him amidst her quiet, unchanging errands, would not show any sign of fear, of concern, of reproach, not even the slightest tear of disappointment, that she would simply *be* there like the house, bright in the daytime and indescribably quiet at night, like the garden, like the humble window by the stairs, even like one of the faithful, familiar, quiet-hearted objects in the house—: that she would be Love, infinite, without care, never less than complete (and hence never wanting)—: Yes, that is how such a homecoming would have to be, beyond all measure, like a blissful death—like resurrection. But I tell you, it is not conceivable. It is not conceivable because it exceeds all powers, the warm nourishing earth powers of the woman as well as, finally, his, the man's, tempestuous powers; for you see, if some day he were to blink and peer out from the dullness of his absorption, if he could see, or just *suspect* in the most hidden corner of his heart, the radiance, the violence — (let me use it in an utterly exalted sense): the sacrifice, the sacrificial ceremony that is constantly being enacted around him — Magda, do you think that would not shock him so profoundly that he would collapse, as the saints collapse when in a cold morning hour of their spirit they become aware of the enormous dimensions of the cross? Don't you see, dear child, even if by some superhuman intervention it were kept hidden from him, argued away and made easy for him, and if he were to make a superhuman effort to believe that this sacrifice that could only be achieved by a continuous miracle of God was simply "Nature," — wouldn't this at least happen: that he would no longer find the strength to take leave, that he would stay, that he would have a gigantic glass ball in his garden and sit there and now see the world inside it dissembling and removing itself, just as he used to see the real world incomprehensibly shifting and disguising itself and growing small before his eyes. Ah, and his beautiful danger would be yearning for him outside and another would set out in his stead and she would love the other. And he would be as a dead man in his garden and a dead man in his house, and the inexpressible love about him would suddenly be like the love one feels for the dead. For where one has come to know his blessedness and wants to remain inside it, that bliss dies, and he, like a fly in a piece of amber, is nothing but a dead little black speck in the beautiful yellow of his dead bliss. — For, to prevent this from happening, to allow him to leave, to allow the beloved to *tell* him to leave as soon as the caravel is set for sailing—: Benvenuta: *what heroes they would both have to be!* The most obdurate heroes. You see: I'm seeing this for the first time: To speak of love is to speak of hardness.

Sister, the sacrifice! The sacrifice is in the world. What is sacrifice? I believe it is nothing other than the boundless, no longer limitable resolve of a human being to reach his purest inner potential — and I will confess to you that I would not have even noticed this word yet if I had not suddenly read it in the work of one who presented it to me—just imagine, to me, of all people—in the context of a tremendous meaning. Its awful diluted Christian usage had made me suspicious of it — and what its archaic fiery original significance may have been is something no one has yet enabled us to grasp. But now it was there, as if grown out of the earth, and was true. — This happened at a very hard time—I tiredly opened the Rundschau and read, among other aphorisms by Rudolf Kassner, the following: *The path from inwardness to greatness leads through sacrifice.*[19] It pierced me through and through. Like a dagger that has been sharpened against you and that the assassin carries for a year beneath his cloak, always holding it ready in his lurking hand: the way such a dagger will finally fly up and out and into the real breast: that's how it struck me. Yes, dearest, that was the problem, I had the inwardness, I possessed it to a high degree—but I possessed nothing else; if my work was to *exist,* the other was needed; *greatness;* and here, suddenly, the bridge had been named—: Where is my sacrifice? Sister, and what will you say when you hear what I learned later, that Kassner had actually *thought of me* when he wrote this line? As a man, he is my friend (in the true and yet not quite literal sense in which that is possible with people who have spiritual trust in each other, though they rarely meet and write even more rarely). As a mind: if he were a hundred and seven years old (instead of about my age) and did not live in the thirteenth district of Vienna (but in the cloud of a mountain peak), that might, more or less, be the tangible equivalent of the awe I occasionally feel at the thought of his inner greatness.

Yesterday he sent me his new book, I read it in the evening—; in it, he lets a probably imaginary uncle of a Lawrence Sterne projected out into pure imagination expatiate, in a most peculiarly eccentric and magnificent fashion, on (of all subjects) what it might be like to be "deep inside, way deep inside" other creatures— —you see, that's how it goes, the result has been all these many pages, and you, Magda, you have to endure them. (Postscript: What follows next came out of sheer fright at this "have to" and out of my reaction against it; as for "Niobe," I have already made up with her in the meantime—so don't worry about her "abandonment.")

Later

What am I saying, my friend, no, no, of course you don't have to, nor, in fact, *should* you any longer. What sort of madness has come over me, how could I erupt like that? Even at night when I lie there without casting forth any fiery matter, it seems to me that the glow of my rebellious lava must hover above me as it does over Stromboli on its element-days. How unfair that all this should come tumbling down on you, so that the good people in your house cannot understand what is happening when they find you so hard to reach through all that invisible rubble and smoke.

And here — if you could only see my lectern standing there, like Niobe; holding up its empty surface as high as it can on its tall stiff legs, epitomizing "abandonment." I will attend to it and turn my thoughts back to my work, and allow only an occasional pause for letter writing, no larger than is needed for a regular-sized letter to fit in, for these are no longer letters but monsters, or letter-titans in revolt against the gods of our hours. But should another of these baby giants burst out and start growing and growing, I shall let it grow here in my drawer, as a kind of journal, and you won't get to see it until later when it is grown up and can open modestly in your hands for half an hour and stay away until you ask for it again. — My God, I hope you forgive me all this pressure.

Et puis je vous écrirai une lettre française pour me plonger dans les vous, rien que dans les vous, vous verrez, ma chère chère Amie.

Later in the evening

May I ask you one thing outright, my confidante? It is this: Did you think it unfair to C. R.[20] that I wrote you a few more lines about her recently? About *myself,* after all, I may tell you everything, but of another only what he happens to be *in me.* Was that perhaps another place where it would have been appropriate to say: but René, how could you? . . . In human affairs I always expect myself to commit some indelicate blunder; I don't know, it seems to me that in such matters only lies are bad or gossip or whatever is still murky and in ferment—; but where an insight has simply settled into a natural clarity, should it not be permissible to share it with a friend, even when it concerns a third person? How little these few words weigh, in the end, against all that remains inexpressible around us, and of which we know that it contains the only completely believable truth. Can you write me a few words about this?

. 21

I just received a good letter from Munich, there was a big performance, at Ruth's friends, of Haydn's children's symphony, complete with masks. An Italian concert master, Gallone, conducted, Ruth played the cuckoo, who, it seems, has to be terribly precise and does not have an easy time of it. What a wondrous, almost dizzying effect that must have had, all those children's voices disguised as birds and mingled with drum, violin, triangle, and clavichord — I picture it as a garden maze of cobweb gray and tinted Venetian glass; but it is probably airier, clearer, and simpler.

On the eighteenth

Yes, on "another star, already in Heaven," it must be so, but tell me, is the cosmos really that old, that we should know each other so boundlessly, from before all conceivable beginnings up to and beyond all conceivable ends, across this bridge of sudden *presence?* I always wanted to imagine, to passionately envision, what it was like when people first encountered bridges across the ancient dangerous rivers. Now I know — (et je comprends que la joie en était telle qu'on ne cessera jamais de danser sur le Pont d'Avignon). Dear heart, imagine, just yesterday I walked to and fro by the edge of such an enormous river and had been walking for years and did not know how to cross it. For no one ever swam across it unassisted. So I waited, sat on the stony bank, did not even see the other shore. And the river roared in its inhuman breadth and it drew me into its noise completely and all that was left of me in its droning was like a small hollow in the middle of a dense stone, for the river drowned out not only every other sound but even my own last, most concentrated silence. But on quieter nights I got up, ran, and called after the ferryman, I thought he must hear me, but the night wind swept over my call, the owl flew right through it, they all denied it. And the ferryman, ever since he had carried the Savior, who was so heavy for him, has been catching up on sleep, knowing there won't be another one coming for some time. That, then, put an end to my chances. But now there is this incomprehensible arc in the early dawn, and my path (how can I believe it) leads so simply, like an easy garden path, directly toward it.

Oh Magda, I believe you when I read your letters, rescuing heart, why else would you have come? A large part of my nature is always opening out in wonder. The amazement I have felt before towers, and again and again, how the stars and my life itself have amazed me. But before you I am not amazed. In you I close my eyes.

We know that we love each other from a time before the earth began, from a childhood before all the ages of being, we love each other from the womb of existence, as the stars would love one another if they knew of their splendor — and now I understand, too, that I did not want to excite any feelings toward you except those of my most spontaneous childhood, that I seek for the purest heart-rays there, to gather them up for you. For a strength, Magda, for an inconquerable strength of heart, from which my true strength for God will only begin to develop, for *that* strength must first be firmly tied to what is human, otherwise it will break in those heights where no one can help it any longer, and wither away in the air. Dear dear girl, may I be granted this, the chance to infinitely, effortlessly love you. May I be granted that, in your hands, the habit of looking on love as a thing to *accomplish* will leave, like an old pain — and that, slowly raising my eyes to look at you, I would no longer know where it had hurt—or what it had been. When I saw others straining toward God, I did not understand it, for though I may have had him less than they did, there was no one blocking the way between him and me, and I could reach his heart easily. It is up to him, after all, to have us, *our* part consists almost solely in letting him grasp us. In its essential soundness, the soul knows no effort toward God; the love of God is the quietly predominant bent of our nature. But with people, effort was all I knew; my heart—in its most festive dress—had to walk back and forth carrying burdens, and thus its rich garments were spoiled. And not only its garments, its gait was impaired; for one who rejoices finds his strength in rejoicing and not in effort. Oh, what will you say when I tell you about *this,* my confidante, this spoilage spreading deep into my soul and all over my body. This sense of being twisted, like a thing that is used to serve a purpose it was not made for. This corrosion or dulling or rusting or misplacing of a tool where it cannot be found. And imagine, dear heart, imagine this calamity befalling the tool (befalling it and persisting) at the moment when it felt strong, straight, finally finished, as it were; as if everything until then had only been a labor preparing it for its purpose—: Now it was ready for the master to use it — oh expectation within a good tool, oh joyous anticipation within the hammer before the first blow, oh workday morning. But then an evil fairy cast a spell upon it. And the tool was taken and carried off in dark pockets; and it was exposed and examined by curious eyes that did not know the purpose it was made to serve; and it was used wrongly and handled wrongly; and it cut the people's hands. Then they got angry and threw it in a corner. And there it remained. And strange things were heaped on top of it.

Dearest, can this be fixed? Perhaps, perhaps not. Probably that is what the silent old master would say if the tool he had once tempered in good, joyful hours were returned to him, damaged. Such a master never says much, nor does he say he is sorry. He has made other tools since then. This one was almost forgotten; now it is there again. That is all. — Oh Magda, if you are not an angel, what more can you do than take it to the old master and say: "Here, try it again—it may be worth it." —? You have angels around you in your music, you have angels around you in your joy, you have angels around you in the purity of your spirit — you have many angels around you: Perhaps they do many things for your sake.

And the tool, too, has an angel, otherwise it would never have turned out *right,* otherwise the old man would not have so thoroughly put his mind to the labor of making it, otherwise it would not have been finished earlier than other tools, so that it could be well used, otherwise it would not have had its humble pride from the beginning: the pride of being a tool. Perhaps all your angels are standing around the veiled angel of the tool, encouraging it and asking to see its face. Ah, of course it has the face of an angel, but it cannot lift its angel's hands off it: In the ardor of its grief they have become like *one* thing— its hands and its face.

You play, and the music drives your love toward me, across the people, wave after wave. Oh love oh beloved—oh influence. Influence across the separation that is coming to an end. How often have I feared the influence of distant people. I believe that distance is a path by which I am more defenselessly accessible than by any closeness. How often something hovers over me, some dark wish, a spell, the cloud shadow of some distant feeling, the coolness of an alien destination. My heart lies exposed in a fearsomely conductive space, I cannot hide it, else I would hide it from the stars as well. How often might there be a struggle, these days, invisible in the air, between your steady influence and the deflecting pull of some alien prompting? Look, dearest, this too: As if it were not enough that you incline the earth toward me and many a wrathful landscape, you must also conquer what opposes me far out in space. For one who is not pure has many enemies everywhere and is not safe from them. Only a pure being walks right through his enemy, shaking him to the core.

Oh purity: Is it still possible? Is it possible still to be pure again? Is there a spring that would not be polluted by washing away one's shamefulness? Can such stained water still show itself in nature, which knows waste and ordure, but no evil, nothing opposed to herself, for she encompasses even what is most alien within her. — Caroline Schelling once wrote in a letter that one could never again expect good fruits from people who had once borne evil ones. When I think of an artist's life, I have always been convinced of this, and was always horrified when I found one who, with an old remnant of strength, would produce some trivial thing on the side, thinking he could again achieve something good whenever it pleased him. As if someone expected to go on writing in beautiful script with a pen with which he had once tried to open a crate. Whoever, in art, has at any time rested content with remaining *below* his greatest achievement, is lost to whatever greatness might have been his. That is why I have always avoided enticing my nature to bear fruit at any price. That is why I have never fertilized it or used any art or ruse against it, or demanded of it that it push forth a plant beneath an up-ended basket in the twinkling of an eye, as the Indian magicians do. I never wanted to perform magic; I never wanted a poison that would make my blood shine like a poisonous flower; never wanted my heart to surge from having some fermenting draught poured into it: When it rose, it rose in accord with the unarguable motions of the sea. When I was inspired, it was the ineffable spirit that inspired me, the glorious spirit that cannot be summoned, nor even implored. Magda, beloved: I speak to God in you and hence am permitted to exalt myself in your heart. Magda, my art is of a splendor unrivaled even by that of the House of David. Magda, the golden pillars stand there like the trees in the forest, and in the pictures of the tapestries there is not a thread that has not been made beautiful by the most genuine color. How God must have stood by me, that I am allowed to say *this*. Here I am pure, for when I was barren, I was prostrate and brought forth nothing.

And had I truly been a stone then, all would have been well. But since I was not a stone, but was merely cast down in my humanness, the great powers that, at other times, I was permitted to sweep along with me now played with me in my wretchedness, as dream images toy with the sleeper. The forces of my childhood have toyed with me, my memories toyed with me, torpid and idle desires toyed with me, my own blood did not know what to do, and toyed with me—: and as happens to toys: this did not make me beautiful, like a worn weapon, but I was damaged, was spoiled: just like a toy.

Do not tell me that a damaged toy has something innocent about it; on the contrary, it takes all the innocence of the child to keep what is dirty and spoiled in the toy free of guilt. If you imagine that object deformed by the hands of an adult, you would turn away from it with horror. And the invisibly play-ing hands that did me such injury were thousands of years old.

And then, you see, there was ugliness. I could not stop before it in my art, for it was not my task to see things face to face, but: from within. For that was the purpose of my sensibil-ity: that I could dwell in ugliness, too. I was not meant to lie down with the leper, I lacked the love, and the canker would not have turned into its blissful opposite beneath me. But I was to go into it completely, all the way into where leprosy's innocence lay, where it still had a childhood; there I had to rally all my strength and powerfully, urgently dissuade the disease from thinking that it was ugly, until it would believe me; for that was its beauty, that it knew nothing of itself—that it just *was*. And in this beauty I gained possession of it, it became substantial and solid, it entered into the world of my art.

Oh dearest, but then I lay there, and the hideousness (to which God has given only its bare, scanty existence while men have lent it a large part of their power)—the hideousness took revenge; saw me lying there, dragged itself nearer, and I fell into its hands a thousand times over.

Magda, you would not believe what ugliness can pass through my soul at the sight of human conditions, not just through my thoughts, but right through my open soul. (That is why I feel such an urgent pull to leave this city, where ugliness has an ancient prerogative, and go out to live among the mani-festations of a guileless nature.) Save me from this too. How often, these days, I find myself promising you that I will never succumb to any thought, any suspicion of a thought, that could not be confessed to you; not that the cruelest, or the most base, the most depraved thought were thereby excluded; only that it should lure me, or tempt me with some hint or entice-ment: *that* is excluded.

Tell me, once all this is written—will I live then, will I die? For this is the testament of all my past and future existence. And who am I that I should be permitted to write it down with a heaving heart, addressing it to you, and seal it with your heart?

On the morning of the nineteenth

Reading this again today, something else occurs to me—that a certain turn in my way of seeing has probably taken me beyond the purely lyrical realm (although actually a large part of my development had to do with the insight that this realm is all-encompassing, that the whole world fits into it). Be that as it may, I feel an urge to create a character who would automatically relieve one of certain problems (recognizing them as his property, so to speak) and snatch them out of my hands the moment they appeared. When Balzac encountered ugliness, he no longer carried it himself, he would respond en grand seigneur, Monsieur de Balzac, by summoning Vautrin or someone else among his creatures, and carefully, firmly lifting the ugly thing with two fingers and bestowing it, quite the creator, magnanimously across the table upon Vautrin.[22] Monsieur de Balzac did not need ugliness; Vautrin needed it, voilà, the matter was settled; the delicious coffee he himself had so lovingly prepared sent up its fragrance, now one could go on writing. Ugliness never had a chance to find itself in Balzac; he disposed of it. And once apportioned to one of his characters, it was immediately no longer ugly but admirable as part of the balance of his imaginary world.

As I think of this: Balzac's famous "lovingly prepared" coffee — ah, where are the times when I brewed my tea "lovingly," with all that knowledge of its ways (as I had learned them in Russia), and with a nearly solemn emotion at having been initiated into the mystery of its transformation — where are those times? How the most trivial undertaking has become a burden to me, an importunity, an impending delay, which I fear, which I want to be done with. Since it became more and more evident that I was *incapable* of love, love began little by little to withdraw from everything, and now whatever needs to be done has a sullen and loveless demeanor; for just being touched by such a loveless one makes it balk and wish it could run away — I don't know, perhaps to the place where all things yearn to be when they are badly off.

Since yesterday a big bowl filled with violets has been standing here. How rarely I dare to fetch flowers; for even the love of flowers has become a strain, their serene, absentminded, dreamy comfort is completely at odds with my strenuous endeavor to cut and arrange them — I find they make inordinate demands. What ghosts everywhere, Magda. Early last spring, after I returned from Spain, it happened that some acquaintances would occasionally bring me flowers. I assure you, they could not have done me a greater disservice. Once (how can one ever forget such a thing!) I had been out of town all day in the country and came back in the evening. Lying in front of my door in the vestibule were a great many flowers, wild ones, brought in from the country, and tall blossoming branches of peach and apple, surely the most wonderful treasures that could be found. Now is this ridiculous or terrible: I worked myself to exhaustion for two hours, trying to find a place for these blossoms in my apartment, there was no vessel tall enough for the heavy, sprawling branches, and when I thought I had found a solution, there were still more flowers left, I discovered them with my light, in the dark, in the most impossible places, on the floor, in armchairs, spread across books, I could not remember having put them there. I searched for another vase, I came back, my light blinded me in the steep darkness, I could no longer find the flowers, I found others. Ah, they looked so tired, as if they had fainted — people had surely carried them in their hands all day, a wilted human warmth clung to their stems; my conscience stirred, I felt one ought to do a lot for them. So I knelt down and put my candle on the floor next to them and wanted to disentangle them and no doubt failed to give them what they needed; when I looked up, the shadow of the branches stood raised up against me on the wall like a huge claw. And when it was finally all done, in passing I overturned the tall vessel with the branches, a flood of water spilled all around — — — Is there a hell, Magda, is there a hell? When someone dreams it, he can still wake up. Those night hours affected me as if the most bitter weeping had been pressed bit by bit into my heart and I was supposed to dissolve it there gradually, and had been given my inmost warmth for *that* purpose only. Forgive my telling you this, oh my dearest.

Abnormal? Certainly. That does not frighten me. I am not afraid of abnormality, for I have no intention of holding on to it, I only want to go through it, weather it. I see it as nothing but a sad need of nature for calculating her way to wholeness and health through all these tangled multiplications: She does the best she can. I believe that as long as one does not misunderstand it and pamper it in oneself, nothing is more infirm than sickness, it wants itself to be unreal, to be gone as soon as something secure can take its place. This is the way I have hoped to accept it, time and again — but how weary weary weary I have grown along the way. As weary in my whole skeleton as boys are when they have growing pains; so weary in walking, so weary in lying down . . . Last summer I spoke to a few doctors here and there, to get rid of at least some of the pain and torment — but I have never been able to communicate with a doctor; they start out with a mistrust of what one presents to them, immediately I have the feeling: A stranger is getting in my way; what is he doing there, between my nature and me? And over his head a glance is exchanged between my nature and myself, ah such a good and familiar glance, Magda, as if a limitless understanding were suddenly possible between us. But imagine that now not even this joy, this confidence, this divine miracle can unite us. Often when my mind is already joyfully turning toward you, the body feels dense with a laggard and sluggish weight, as though it knew nothing and could no longer be taught. If I were yet to soar to the height of another heart, would the body be able to follow? It used to be carried away so easily, and there were times when I knew both states at once: its juicy vegetative gladness, and the weightless, vibrant serenity of the soul.

Ah my close, closest, inmost friend, if only I did not have to do this and that and see this person and read those letters and suddenly even go out to my silly little restaurant: if God would only understand my plight and feed me right here unobtrusively with the help of a raven, and I could just keep sitting here like "St. Jerome in his cell," writing to you. Then, when the raven comes with his lovely round little world-bread, I just nod in a way that can be grasped by such a bird, and say: "Thank you, put it over there, please!" — — and . . . forget it. Forget it, dearest, and yet live and go on living a thousand times in my trust in you. I feel: that you are *there:* this alone should be air and food and drink for me. What early and beautifully, purely defined memories you have — I don't think I have any reaching that far back, or else they looked blurred like drawings on blotting paper, or as empty as enormous enlargements of tiny Kodak pictures. But you have memories almost like Tolstoy's, I always thought his were the product of obstinacy, that he *wanted* them that way and scrubbed and scrubbed himself until the contours of his past clearly stood out through his skin. But your memories are just as convincing, yet they lie there in such dear simplicity, just as they are, like a linden leaf in a book, and right next to them that little song that first made you cry because it is sad about itself and no one can help it.

Such a one-horse carriage, my God (I hope it didn't have little lanterns on top of it?), no, I don't want to hear any more about it, for I never had one, and yet I had an inexpressible longing for it. (And you see, for *that,* after all, it is much too late now.)

And that you should have actually played before Fräulein Hueber! When I first read: "Olga," I felt a tiny pang inside me. But when I come to think of it, imagine—I just don't remember whether that was her name. Such, then, is my disposition toward fidelity. (A closer examination might reveal that I was only in love with "Hueber," or perhaps with no more than that lovely "ue" — poor me.) The other day, when I wrote you about her, amazed even to remember her, she appeared to me as something between a specter and a legend—and now it turns out that she really existed, exists in some fashion even now. How miraculous all this seems. That we both should have known her — if this were a story, it would be all wrong. People would say: Why, of course! But we have no story, we only have this our joy, which God brought forth at the very beginning of Creation along with all the other things, and no one ever dared to make use of it, for it looked perfectly improbable: And so it came to us fresh from Paradise.

Last night, gently waking up from time to time, from a sleep that was peculiarly spacious (I lay as if in the midst of a lofty sleep-creation), I wrote down on slips of paper many things I absolutely had to tell you, on the spot. The thoughts on the one-horse carriage, for instance, were written then—and some I can no longer decipher.

It says here: Flowering tree, tentative flowering, that recovers its roots in you. Hence all this deep-dug subterranean: only to hide and plant myself more firmly in your dear soil.

It also says: So courageous are you toward me —

Then it says: Love, love, isn't it too much for you? — And then just single words, whose meaning I have yet to recall.

Toward evening

Dear heart, what was it? After two, I came back home from lunch, opened your telegram: It seemed as though you were saying something fearsome, darkly anxious in your sleep. What was it that moved you? Your message went off at 12:05; that was just when I was writing all that fearsome business about the flowers — did you feel it? Now I'd rather not send it to you at all. But look, it's no worse than the rest, and besides, it's in the past now, and in the way I relate it to you, next to other, less weighty things, next to my confidence, on all sides surrounded by it, by you — this, I believe, should show you how calmly detached from it I am, shouldn't it? I got a few things ready for the mail, then I went to my little post office and wired you this: All well while wiring long letter will send tomorrow stop otherwise well enough. *This* is the letter, it will go off tomorrow morning at the latest, and that I called it "long" is almost a lie, for it is length personified. I was about to write "long long," which would have been much closer to the truth, but suddenly I remembered that this sort of thing is a waste of money in a telegram, so I swallowed back the second "long," but I never understood the two or three sous this was supposed to save me, since no one gave them to me. That's how it always is.

Finally, let me tell you about my post office, for that is as far as I can ever go toward you; then I have to entrust to others all that is reaching out to you, here, in such solitude and fullness of heart. Now, you have no idea — how shall I put it? — what a frugal little household they make of post offices here, with eternally warmed-up pens and blotters; absolutely nothing gets lost; behind the counter gates lots of females and little pneumatique boys* with dreamily absent eyes and open mouths, so that one is tempted to roll up one's card and put it right in there; a lot could be said about the ladies, and if it were up to them, they'd be the main topic of my report. But for now, I will limit myself to another creature into whose being I recently happened to stray for a brief moment, not a dog, but almost. For dogs aren't allowed in, but if one has a dog and has to leave it outside, and it sits there with its head cocked sideways, wondering why its master sends so many wrong bodies out before he himself returns to his unsurpass-able rightness — it can happen that "the creature" opens the door (that object of fervent hope, the sacred door) just a bit to let the dog know that there is still hope and that he is protect-ing its master inside; this lasts only a moment, then you see the creature back at his place, and the creature turns out to be a very small old man with strained red eyes — and the place is a very small old desk outside the counters, close to the inner entrance door. I assume this being was not wasted before he was put to his present use, which consists of cleaning up in the morning, or contriving to do so, by searching for three or four rags he's left lying in various places, finding them, examining them sternly through his glasses, and depositing them a little further away. There comes a moment when this unrest is no longer compatible with the elevated position of the sun; from now on you can be sure to find him at his desk, where I have known him to be occupied with three tasks: The principal one

* Pneumatic tubes were used in Paris to convey short messages. [Tr.]

is to salvage from the waste baskets (the investigation of which forms part of his morning exercises) damaged letter cards that might still lead to the rescue of an unredeemed postage stamp, and to reconstitute them, shred by shred, with a meticulosity beyond compare. If he were producing this out of nothing, it would be Creation itself. That's number one. — Secondly, he reads the newspaper, about which there is nothing more to be said; but thirdly, he reads a large quantity of quite old-fashioned and also very small volumes, the content of which I am frankly rather curious to learn. Now these three activities—as if the whole fragile little package were about to be shipped far, far away—are separated one from the other by pieces of dense sleep as if by cotton rolls and cotton walls, so that they cannot knock against each other. There he sleeps, tiny, his old sleep-face on the desk, as if he had fallen asleep as a boy on his school bench and not woken up since. — But what I was getting at was this: He slept, even though there was all sorts of commotion in the rooms, people coming and going, you could even hear the rather loud and authoritarian voice of the office supervisor addressing a gentleman in the back; my business was done — the gentleman left, other people left, I left, and just then, as I was leaving, from the motions and voices behind me, I more or less gathered the following: The supervisor wanted his gentleman back again. In such a case one would use, well, you can imagine whom — ah, dearest, I turned around: There he stood already, the old man, on the threshold, on the threshold of reality; the office had thrust him into the world (newborn, as it were), there he stood, filled with an inexpressible longing for a gentleman whom he had never seen: It was almost sleep all over again. From his point of view (and I saw it from his point of view, I can't help it, from *inside* him) it was for two or three seconds optically correct to regard all the people one saw from the back as having just left

97

the office, not one of them surpassed the others by the slightest probability — like the results of a single cause, they all proceeded eternally from the existence of this post office. The old man stood baffled in front of this abstraction; inadvertently he drew back into himself, to that place where just seconds ago he had enjoyed all the certainties of sleep, way back inside — and now it was unavoidable that he would meet me there—: We were both delighted. I very nearly went back inside with him, but I changed my mind (all this took no more than a moment's time) and quickly helped him select the most likely among the many steadily receding backs. And now: Good night. So many things I've told you. You have my telegram, you may also have the little letter I sent you yesterday, or you'll have it tomorrow morning at the latest—. And then, dearest you have — — — *all the rest.*

On the twentieth, early morning

Beloved, your letter, I am writing you this in the midst of reading it, to tell you that it has come. To tell you that I cannot read it *all at once,* because it is overwhelming my heart so violently — where you write about roses, I had to stop, as when one runs against the sea wind, one thinks one could take all of it into one's lungs, and suddenly one can't go on — what to do in the face of infinity? — I feel as if I were hearing the language of human beings for the first time, you see, I only know it from the great eternal poems and from my own, struggling ones. Never has language seemed wondrous to me in another, oh how you make me love language. Do we not speak to each other as the stars speak to the earth and the earth to the stars? Just that our speech is not silence, not cosmic silence, but language, the language of human beings.

I send you all these pages without continuing to read yours now, I'll be interrupted in a moment, the femme de ménage — and then, I am so drawn to you that I must do something definite, demonstrably visible in your direction, and that will be to step out beneath a morning sky that is clearing up its long, gray indecision and carry this letter to my little post office, which seems infinitely reliable to me, now that you have gotten to know it a bit.

You dearest dearest

Rainer Maria

Rilke to Benvenuta

On the morning of the eighteenth

Your two letters and the card of the 16th. — An utterly new jealousy is developing, not between this page and the work sheet, no, it's quite an exuberant one that I'm sure no one has ever thought of. Imagine: It's between the journal-letter for you that is slowly gaining weight in the drawer and this incidental page through which I shall quickly step out just to tell you: Love, love, love —

Has anyone ever been able to say how present the miraculous is in the world, not just here and there and not just at some goal, not just in reach of our hands—but present inside us, in every cell of our being; and when we are suddenly sure of its omnipresence — behold, it is transformed from the incomprehensibly extraordinary thing that it is into something sacredly natural — into the law, without which we would not even exist.

You have flowers, many flowers around your breakfast table, good that you described it (how I saw and felt that table, what comfort it gave me in my travail — there is nothing less mysterious than the ins and outs of a breakfast a man has prepared for himself — he should never know how such things come about); yes, your yellow tulips, dear heart — I felt a real longing to know whether you have flowers — and I confess I was fairly close to having roses sent through Franziska Bruck to welcome you at your arrival in the Grunewald. I forbade myself this for several reasons, but mainly I told myself: how much of me will actually be reflected in these roses, no matter how urgently I impress upon good old Franziska B. that it should be these and these — either she has them or she doesn't, and in the end she will act in my so-called interest, according to the dictates of her ambition, her zeal, and her curiosity. And would these be *my roses*?! — And doesn't all this bloom for you, incomprehensible one, all these letters I'm writing for you, are they not your flowers, is there even *one* which you did not bring forth, heart-sun — and are you not calling and calling many more for which my earth is too small, oh radiant voice. A botanist would have a hard time with them, for they all bear your name, how could he distinguish them? They are like the stars, whose real names are simply the inexpressible names of the sky, and not the ones we give them.

Geneva — dear God, Magda, I have never seen my valise look like this; I just glanced in its direction, it penetrated my eyes through the curtain, feeling empty as never before in its life, and demanded to be packed right away; I'll really have to hold on to it now, otherwise it will take off to Geneva without me some day, empty, together with the traveling blanket that lies on top of it. Precious heart, is it really possible? My letter, one of them, I'm no longer sure which, will by now have given you this answer, and I'm sure you can feel it as well. Oh *feel* it.

And how marvelous that it is a city where I have never been. In the beginning I would like to be with you only in places that are completely new to me, as radiantly new as all this, until, gradually, the old ones, too, shall pass into *our our* glory, as if resurrected, without turning back.

Rainer Maria

Give yourself to whatever absorbs and fulfills you, my dear heart, don't think you have to answer each one of my letters, just *be* there, *be there*.

I, too, have been approached by the concert agency Hermann Wolff, asking me to give a reading in Vienna some time in 1914/15. *Warsaw,* unfortunately, has never asked me (I only remember it from an early morning ride, after an endless night of traveling, in transit from one train station to another, before starting on an endless day-trip into the endlessness of Russia. Verhaeren recently came back from there and had beautiful things to tell; but since he had been in Moscow and Petersburg too, those memories, especially the ones of Moscow, were by far the most prominent.) As for the request from Vienna, I'm going to decline it: For one, I don't want to give public readings any more, unless there were a particular subject I really wanted to talk about; and also, if I did come back to Vienna, I wouldn't want to rob my loyal old Hugo Heller of his benign view of the world and its ways by reading at any other place than his: Mine was the first such reading he offered years ago.

R .

Rilke to Benvenuta

Paris
February 20, 1914

Dearest heart,
    I was walking along one of the most beautiful avenues in the world, lined with chestnut trees, where I walk to and fro in the morning almost completely alone (oh *avenues,* who has ever felt deeply enough *what* that is), continuing your letter as I

walked, and reading it to the end with the dear, the endless feeling that this end cannot interrupt my awareness, my knowledge of you, raised my eyes and, behold: Where were you not? Is there a place where you would be absent, you beautiful meaning and sense of the world, through which I want to reach the higher senses of the universe which we cannot yet grasp. Oh my heart feels like a spring, and next to it lies my old deep sullen well, let it; I'm not drawing from it these days. Oh, I don't know quite why, I pass it a little shyly, a hedge of wild roses hides me from it, how graciously they cast out their tendrils — I turn away, I kneel: ah, and my spring leaps into my hands.

Would that I were young enough to love you, so that there were no place in my body too heavy, too dense, too dull for the spirit of my love: Oh, when, in such a spirit, the gods entered a human body, it was always a hale body, invented for this purpose alone, they could be sure of shining through every part of it. But I, in this used, somewhat worn body—. Yes, dear heart, I too would like it if you called me by a name that is mine without my really knowing it, as when in the Bible someone is suddenly accosted by a name that is not the one by which his mother called him — nor is he told that this is a name like the previous one; no, what it says in the Bible is — I call thee thus: *for thou art* . . . I don't quite remember my other first names, never found them interesting, loosely assorted as they were from the immediate neighborhood of relatives for reasons of polite consideration; not borrowed from any older traditions, which would add to the name a sound of something one doesn't know and that yet belongs to one from God knows where. But I will take a look in my birth certificate (a touching document, frightfully old and all weak in its creases, as if I had been born sometime around 1740). Occasionally I almost believe that I *was*. For there is nothing that puts me so at a loss as does our time by some of its (perhaps its best) qualities. It often seems to me—I just wrote this to Herr von Schlözer,[23] who sent me the letters of his great uncle, the ambassador in Rome around 1860—that what is old-fashioned now was once truly "a time"; I can sense another one coming again, in a mighty Russia of the future—but that ours is just a sort of rapid escape from not having any time. — That is why it may be truly dangerous to raise the vibrations of *our* days into a permanently exalted sphere that perhaps has no intention for us other than to outlast us deep inside its greatest glory.

But what is all this I am writing, dearest, when I wanted only to write of the *place* around which our first earth-plans may mutually sustain each other in a delicate floating balance (somewhat like that of a swarm of butterflies I once observed for an entire summer in a beautiful park in Bohemia— imagine: gaily circling about the roundly blooming crowns of high-stemmed heliotrope shrubs); the place then. It could, may, can, should be *any* place you choose, to make it effortlessly compatible with your professional arrangements and itinerary. Against Munich, however, I would have one objection: that there I could not be *quite* as new and free as everywhere else, for naturally I would see Ruth and not remain totally outside the circumstances that are part of her manyfold little life, and in which she includes me with perfect ease and confidence on my rare visits. There, too, I would have to give some kind of explanation concerning my trip. But if that location should be the most suitable for you, we could settle for a place near Munich; Würzburg, for example, which I do not know, with its beautiful park and its shimmering Tiepolos, and where, I imagine, one could find a comfortable and not too new hotel; or perhaps a smaller town in the countryside. God, I have lost my last traces of geography, I can't think of a single place; ever since I've learned of the one that is your heart, I can't take any of the others quite seriously. But you *know* your geography, so you decide — and I even suspect you're good with figures (oh dear, I'm not), — please don't startle me with too many such qualities, otherwise too much respect will enter into my simple-hearted admiration. — That you wrote "eighteen" days, that by now they are fewer and that each day makes it one whole day less; that you let me hope (I say only: hope!) that, after that first place, we might still do something together (of our own) — Dearest, dearest, all this I'm not even thinking yet, I only carry it at the bottom of every thought.

Rainer

Now you help yourself with the little pinwheel. Well, if one can rely on a little pinwheel for help! . . . May you be well rested, no longer tired, I know those pains so well! (I will have this letter registered after all, otherwise I'll be worried that such a little one will simply get lost after such big and heavy ones.)

February 20

How exact and fitting is your account of the old lady, it all adds up without remainder, like an angelic reckoning. Beautiful, too, that she gave you her name, thus convening her entire family, with the authority an old lady has over such things, to examination, redress, and apology. You see, that is precisely it, you dear, dear soul: if people would only look at one another that way, directly out of their profoundest grandeur, blissfully or wrathfully—: Why, one after the other would be frightened, say his name, and change. But as it is—how do they look at each other? . . . and then all the bonbons or marbles or what-

104

ever they are just go on rattling in those thin bags (which are rightly served by their name, *ridicule*).

༘

Benvenuta to Rilke

Thursday morning, February 19

I had a dream, Rainer, that was too strange to keep from you. Just listen! — We were sitting opposite one another, you and I, in a large, somewhat bare room with light gray walls; you were tired and said with an alien voice that was not yours at all: "Do you know what I once wanted to do? To let one of those 'scientific' types unravel my soul, dissect it—I think it's called analysis." That's what you said — I leaned far over to you, took both your hands firmly in mine and said—no, screamed with a heartrending fear that was its own unquestionable evidence: "Rainer, if *I* may beg something of you, don't do it, don't do it! Rainer! Rainer!" — Suddenly your eyes turned bright and you said, all youthful and glad: "Now I don't want to any more—Benvenuta, I *don't* want to." And tears just poured from my eyes.

Can you tell me how or whether all this is related to you? Whether it had even the slightest breath of reality in your thinking? It must, I see this dream image too vividly in my mind for it to be just a dream. Please tell me soon. It stirred me very very deeply. — Now that we are in dreamland, I suddenly recall something I haven't thought of for months, the strangest dream I have ever had (before the one about you). I must tell it to you as it stands before me, newly risen.

There was a large half-lit room like a huge tower room, square, with powerful stone walls — a dark heavy river slowly streamed in from somewhere and disappeared in a deep place with stairs leading down, the antechamber of the underworld. The tower room, however, had four windows: one facing the forest, one the mountains, one the sea — and through the fourth one could gaze into the life of our time. But Charon stood immobile at the entrance and saw them all coming: children, men, youths—old men and women too, many women. They walked silently and humbly down the steps into an unexplored darkness. I myself at one of the great windows rang the bells, deep wonderful bells, and thought: "When— when!" And then boats came across the sea, steered by men with dark gold helmets, and there was a woeful radiance above them and above the sky, which shone with a reddish glow between heavy clouds. Had they set out to raid the house of death? Something dark slid before the window through which one saw them coming, a cry was heard, then everything was quiet. And I rang the bells and thought: "When—when."

But suddenly it happened: Through the fourth window one had a view of a broad, noisy street; in the midst of many hurrying people walked a little girl (I saw her clearly) in a red dress. She was carrying a doll in her arms, was jostled from behind, and the doll fell to the ground. As the child lovingly bent down to pick it up, a team of wildly stampeding horses ran over her little body. She did not scream, she merely toppled and fell — — and a hundred people were already there to help her. One of them held her in his arms — — and Charon stepped forward slowly, as if waking from sleep, to look at her. The child was bleeding, her little head hung to one side, she was dying—and yet she was smiling, imagine— she was smiling, and then, Rainer, then everyone saw it: Charon wept. Like shining stars, tears welled from his rigidly staring eyes, which were waking to life and to heavenly compassion. Suddenly there was a swelling, rushing sound in the air. My bells swung high above it like the flight of birds — but from the depths they were all coming back, all of them, children, men, old men and youths, and many, many women. The rushing sound and the ringing grew stronger and stronger and finally became a single choral of rejoicing: Behold, a child has redeemed the world! — —

I am sending you this letter and yesterday's together. Receive them in the spirit in which I bring them to you. Everything is so good and clear today, and cheerful, too, for the little pinwheel is telling me all sorts of nice things for you. Just now it is dancing gracefully, gaily lifting its four red and white little legs in the air. Dearest, I am taking all this here to the post office. Perhaps there'll still be a letter from you today?

Magda

Rilke to Benvenuta

February 21, Saturday

Oh Benvenuta, thou Benvenuta unto me, do you understand this? Are we going ever more deeply into the miraculous? Your dream of Wednesday night! Do you realize that was the night of which I wrote to you that I lay there as if in the midst of a dream-creation, indeed in a nameless spaciousness of sleep, in which the spirit, open-eyed, feathered in the colors of sleep, circulated in a deep night-wakefulness—; the same night when from time to time I wrote messages to you on small slips of paper, thinking this could not wait, you must know it immediately; the same night when, in that transparent feeling, I experienced all the hundred fatigues of my body, unappeased, each one a complete, each a hopeless fatigue in its own place: not that they rested—; rather, as is done by way of testing colors in some needlework, each one had lying next to it a soft silken strand of its complementary repose—, as though each strand was to be worked thread by thread into the dun material by a loving hand, in thoughtfulness, gentleness, and ineffable peace, sometime, soon: There I lay, you see, and no kindness was done unto me; on the contrary, my complete exhaustion lay in my bodily consciousness like a number with very many digits, but above it, everywhere in my mind, there emerged the sacred pledge, the promise of such an indescribable well-being that I would not have dared to move for fear of dispelling the miracle that was coming so close. I know that even in the morning I got up very very carefully, amazed at the greatness of the night that had just slipped away — it make me think of the promises in the Bible, where something not yet existent is given unto the seed of a very old man, over and beyond him, generations, an inexhaustible future in which, for a long time, he finds it impossible to believe; or of the dream visions in Dante's Vita Nuova; never had I experienced anything like this temple-sleep through which a god had walked, not yet acting as if *preparing* for action, looking about, planning. — And you, loving heart, you dreamed during *that* night.

It was when I was writing the last passages of Malte Laurids,[24] shaken in every fiber of my body by all that I had summoned up in the way of vital and mortal pain — and I would not have been able to go on if I hadn't from time to time comforted my face with my two hands, telling myself: Patience, friend, this is the limit, after this you will stop writing. (Ah, stop writing? Did I mean stop living? I think so.) That was exactly four years ago. That was when I first learned of psycho-analysis, from a close friend,[25] on whom this discipline had dawned with the unexpected impact of a profound upheaval in the midst of completely unrelated activities, a most multifarious and finely tuned mind who had already been able to draw all sorts of sprouts and branches from this new phenomenon, though not yet a full-blown flower. Then he left Paris, I did not see him for a long time, but I learned that after going through an apprenticeship he had begun to treat patients; now he is actually planning to take up the study of medicine, so as to continue his treatments and research on a much broader basis. — During these last difficult years, then, there really were two or three times when I was on the verge of undergoing an analysis, be it by a friend, be it by Prof. Freud himself; the last time, in the fall of 1912, it was almost a choice: analysis or a trip to Spain. You know that I chose the trip. When I attended the convention for a day last summer in Munich, it was in order to see Freud and a Swedish physician, Dr. Bjerre, with whom I already had an indirect contact through the intermediation of Swedish friends. These men were important and significant for me, their whole orientation and method certainly represents one of the most essential movements of medical science, indeed of that *human* science that does not yet properly exist. But that *for me* there could be nothing more disastrous, more deadly, than to expose myself to the influence of such a treatment even to the slightest degree: This was, fortunately, perfectly clear to me already. The more I learned of the intentions, successes, and advances of analysis, the more I had to realize that it could not but have an undermining effect on an existence that owed its strongest impulses precisely to the fact *that it did not know itself,* that by its own heavy and blessed secret it was inexhaustibly part of all the secrets of the world and even of God, and was secretly and magnanimously sustained from there. Dear heart, dear dear girl, there was a moment when I adjured and cried out against myself in defense, as you did in your dream, when I came to realize that I had so intrusively tried to ferret out my confusion, knowing full well that God, the most impenetrable, is my confusion, and no one else. Sister, I attained a new awe before my inwardness when I became aware that I must not *let myself be guided into it,* that I possess it only when I lie down, poor as I am, across its threshold, as a lover lies in all his indigence before the unexplored heart of the beloved, upon which he has no claim, unless, incomprehensibly, the lovely one were to come out of her own accord. And I promised myself to suffer even more than I have already suffered and to drown in my increasing pain rather than presumptuously insist on seeing the powers that determine my lot for me deep deep within: *For therein, too, lies my power, that I do not impede the most secret powers within me.*

Benvenuta, thou Benvenuta unto me since the beginning of time. Do we understand one another?

Yesterday evening—despite the fact that, after your letter, I read something very beautiful—a truly fainthearted feeling came over me. May I tell you that, too, my sister? — I felt as though I would not be able to travel at all, it is a foolish nervousness; after four months in this cell, I sometimes feel like the prisoner who is released and grows dizzy at the thought of stepping out among all those things and events—. Then I somehow physically lose my courage. I wanted to go to sleep, couldn't deal with anything, even going to sleep seemed too much for me—let alone traveling! Oh scold me, dear heart—but this, too, suddenly frightened me—that what is already such a big grown-up surging within us should turn into a small helpless child again, born into the visible, in a strange city. Was it because I don't own a "blue jacket," though I often owned one in the past—?

During the day, after writing to you, it almost made no difference to me which city it would be: Now I had to picture to myself how easily an essentially innocent but clumsy circumstance might compromise our meeting; that one should prepare it more carefully, protect it; that it should at least be the way it is in my room, where, to a degree, it is possible to prevent disruptions and accidents. Where I could say to all things: Ssh! she's coming, or say nothing at all, but the stillness of all things would grow greater and more certain around my clamoring heart. — Outside, how can one teach this to such a city? And yet again there are reasons why I would almost not want to see you for the first time here, in this place of painful exhaustion.

I must further confess to you that perhaps ten days ago it occurred to me to travel into the Umbrian countryside to meet the approaching spring, since here it reminds me too much of other springs, and sometimes a great yearning for hour-long walks in the country can take hold of me, as if for a counterbalance to the constant inner movement, — (I don't know how early one could go down there without fear of still finding winter or a relapse of winter there — just to make sure, I wrote to someone who should know); and when, a few days later, you mentioned Geneva, dearest, there rose a kind of hope in me, immoderate as I am, as if I could see us sitting around a table in a hotel in Geneva, the four of us—that is, your and my "black bags" beside and hence between us, having been granted both seat and vote and drawn into the most serious council — saw before us your yellow book, from which I read out loud to you some indescribably melodious names, Perugia, Assisi — — Dear heart, there I was, loafing about in such frivolousness, and didn't want to tell you anything about it. Only, when you happened to mention Geneva, it all acquired a kind of fantastic probability — (or am I once again completely outside all geography?). As far as I'm concerned, it isn't yet possible for me to foresee whether I would do well to go to Umbria and then spend a month or two there or whether it wouldn't be better to return, from wherever it may be, to my lectern and desk (my black bag, of course, unimaginative as it is and exhausted by lean years, quickly votes in favor of the latter — but you should know that I often consult it only in order to suddenly do the opposite of what, in the dry manner of an irritated governess, it advises me to do) — so I actually don't know anything yet whatsoever; since my obstinate staying here has led me to such indescribable places — should I not (when the times comes . . .) quietly continue? Somehow I'm attached to it, attached to this much distrusted room, though it's been a frequent torment to me, I feel a new kind of leniency toward it, now that such letters have been written in it. Ah, my heart, as soon as we have met, I'm sure everything will proceed quite easily and by itself from the most willing future. There I go, troubling you with this weakness, page after page (I'm sure you're tired of reading about it); I have no excuse, you see, except perhaps that I really am somewhat suspended between two lives: an old, past life that is beginning to seem unbelievable to me — and a life — — — about which nothing more can be said than that I can hardly believe in it yet.

(Doesn't all this interfere with your plans? Be ruthless, please, as you must be in the interest of your goals and endeavors.)

Dearest, your other dream: Do you know what that is? — That is *the most beautiful* of the "Stories of God." It is not in my book, for I did not write it: *You* dreamed it. And that it is so — in this there is a great and splendid, incomprehensible justice.

I'm taking this to the post office.

Magda, how my hands yearn for your hands; they don't even feel like hands any more when they touch each other — not until they find themselves in your dear hands do they hope to recover their mysterious fate.

Rainer Maria

Give me the Beethoven letters until we see each other. How strangely beautiful that, for all my desires to have them, I always felt somehow prevented from ordering them. I only know those that are reflected in Bettina von Arnim's books. (Three of them, addressed to her, in "Ilius Pamphilius und die Ambrosia," a later correspondence between Bettina and the young Philipp Nathusius.)

Benvenuta to Rilke

February 20, 1914

Dearest!

Today I bought the Book of Hours and a number of your other books. The friendly assistant in the store handed me a printed sheet "in case you are seriously interested in Rilke," as he put it, half superciliously, half obligingly. I had to laugh: Rainer, "arranged" in the order of his works! "No," I replied, "I have no further interest in Rilke," with a radiant smile that made the young man quite confused: "Please use this silk ribbon to tie this bouquet of violets onto the books. Like that — thank you!" — "May I perhaps send you a catalogue or the prose volume for you to examine?" the young man continued, undeterred. "It is called "The Notebook of — —" But I pressed three violets into his hand and carried you and the bouquet home. Now you are here — your past and present, those are my flowers now — and the embodiment of spring, the bouquet of violets, envelops them. — What you wrote me earlier about Greco: I wanted to answer you long ago, but other things came in between. At any rate, two years ago I knew nothing about him; then, in Munich, I saw the two paintings. I felt attacked by an almost physical pain—there is such hopelessness in it, in the faces of the people, and of the god. No, dearest, music is not like that, believe me. Music is always resurrection, and even at its most painful it is still a storm that wants to free the heavens from the burden of towering clouds. But a crucifixion? No! Not the blood of Christ, but the angel who flies toward him, the angel who helps Magdalene, that is music, Rainer! You don't quite know it completely, and yet: Who has ever written about music as you have? You have a sense and a dormant feeling for it.

You know— —now that I've just received your letter, I feel like running to my little post office and wiring you: Come! Will you answer me with a single word: "Yes"? . . . . You present everything to me so clearly, but it seems painful from *your* point of view; so I would like to find the lighted path. Oh, Rainer, the sailor's bride! How simply this could be resolved, how humanly and understandably. Why sacrifice? When he would come, she would simply be there, and be his as a matter of course, having waited for him, his nourishing earth. How he would carry this knowledge within himself and she within herself, so that there would be neither sacrifice nor a "dead bliss"; how staying or leaving would be simply decided, star-like, for in both of them, necessity would imply neither renunciation nor leavetaking, only calm and storm, time and silence, for God would have fashioned all these into one thing: Love,

114

averted and released from all that human beings mean when they utter this word, which has almost become unholy on their tongues.

You believe that sacrifice is the illimitable commitment to one's purest inner potential. In your art you have recognized this purest possibility, but in your humanity you deem yourself (so often!) small, powerless, burdened, incapable. Just see how abundantly blessed you are, have faith in your humanness too, it may be just this faith that will be your "bridge" to everything from which you still feel excluded. Courage of will and faith in one's own future . . . . . .

Rainer, perhaps we'll no longer need these inhospitable letter sheets, perhaps a great loving moment of silence will mean more than all words.

Dear Rainer, come soon!

Magda

Rilke to Benvenuta

Sunday

Oh, Magda, there was much I wanted to write you, and it will come in time — but at the moment, how can I think of anything but this: You will be in Paris? Once again you send me a few ready-made dates, all shiny new — dear heart, all those holidays marked in red, Easter, Whitsun, whatever their names are, none of them can measure up to these. What a magnificent calendar you have made, dearest, more beautiful than Pope Gregory's, a heart-year, people will reckon by it a thousand years hence, and then the good Lord will spend the whole day with them every Sunday and tell them stories already the night before.

Just recently I wanted to ask you, in a lighthearted moment, whether you really thought you could settle things with your Paris agent by mail, for all times to come; and I wanted to confess that I found this extremely risky, considering the overwhelming importance of that city. Meanwhile you will have discovered by reading the letter I sent you yesterday (and my letters in general) how quickly such lighthearted moments pass for me — will you scold me, put me to shame?

I deserve it more than I know, but you see, you are dealing with a convalescent who is taking his first cautious steps into joy, gently leaning on your shoulder; he easily loses heart in his unaccustomed confidence, and so he needs to sit down or even turn back, and the moment he is seized by a spell of dizziness or is stabbed by a twinge of pain or alarmed by some other unexpected sensation, his courage is gone. For all this reminds him all too closely of the unexpected changes and feelings which the sickness used to visit upon him from one moment to the next, and since they were his only source of strength for so long, the strength of his recovery now makes him believe he is sick. Is this it? Am I making it look too good, too excusable? Dear, dear heart, I pass, without asking, from your kindness to your patience as if from one room to another, as though I were allowed to go everywhere and hold my face close to the flowers you put there, and stroke the silk of your dear feelings with my hand. Oh my precious one, I will never be able to tell you all the things you are doing for me, it is in-inexpressible, unless from now on God instructs all the gardens you walk through to tell you about it in their most blissful way; unless the stars you look up to deliver it, pure and heavenly, into your heart; unless all things love you, Magda, and tenderly flatter your hands with it when you touch them; there's no other way for you to learn nearly enough about it. For you do not *know* what it means to me that I will sit near you while you read, that I will watch you as you sew bright silken flowers on white batiste — and when I then take a book and read to you and can no longer look at you — there will nevertheless be no place in my whole being that does not *know* that you are sewing silk flowers on white batiste and that is not thereby provided with a sacred protection that will make it almost impossible for it to remain mortal. — Many years ago I spent a winter far down south in a villa from which one had a view of the sea across the evergreen gardens: There were only four of us: three women of various ages and I; an old lady; the hostess, a widowed woman, no longer young; and a lovely young girl.[26] The hostess was the sister of a deceased woman who had been a motherly friend to me; thus I was not really close to her, and my relationship to the other two guests was also no more than that pleasant ease in giving and taking that develops among people who have cordially shared a house for a while, without knowing how deeply one is really touched by that genuine sympathy. There were evenings (not many visitors came) when we got together in the large studio, near the fireplace, the ladies with their needlework, I with a book — and it always ended with the young girl peeling an apple for me—. Would you believe it, Magda, that for years and years I was nourished by this apple which I did not have to provide for myself; by that evening hour; by something which the proximity and gentle preoccupation of these three women had established and stored within me?: Even much later, long after I was back in Paris, there was still a supply of . . . (what?) of composure, of comfort, of a cooling and soothing inner influence that, I could tell, had its source in that time; and this

117

supply was so real, so tangibly stored up inside me, that I could almost see it decrease with my daily and ever more anxious consumption. — And *all it was was a gesture:* and yet it sustained me for years, just imagine— —

My heart, when your letter came today, I went to work at once . . . (looking up the old people or the good old lady with whom you might stay—is that what you think?) no: right here at home, an enormous dusting job, as if you'd be coming in half an hour. The femme de ménage had planned a trip to the country, she had come earlier and left very early, I was gloriously alone — when, out of the blue, this old passion came over me. You should know that it was very nearly the greatest passion of my childhood, even my earliest connection to music, for our piano was part of my dusting precinct, it was one of the few objects that lent themselves readily to dusting and yet never turned out to be boring in their response to the dust cloth's zeal; on the contrary, it would suddenly hum so metallically and yield beautiful dark reflections the more one exerted oneself. What a variety of experiences might have been involved in this? Pride, for one, supplied the necessary equipment—the big apron and the protective little chamois gloves on the busy hands. One would respond to the friend-ship of these well-rested, well-treated objects with a certain impish propriety. — And even today, I must confess, as order was restored around me here and as the vast black surface of the desk (it belongs to Rodin, incidentally, and has been merely lent to me, for years), about which everything revolves, gained a sort of new awareness (having become more reflec-tive) of the high, light gray, almost cubelike room, it affected me as though what had occurred were not just simply and literally a superficial event, but that something beautiful had happened from soul to soul, as when the emperor washes the feet of the old men or St. Bonaventura the tableware in his monastery.

Now it has grown so late over this unexpected resurgence of my passion (for which you are to blame) that I must quickly finish to go and eat in my little restaurant — and I'll take this letter with me to the post office, for it's sad having to walk the streets on a Sunday afternoon, with all the stores closed and the people let out into that peculiar emptiness, in search of invisible amusements.

Your old lady—I wonder whether she still exists? Surely in the provinces she does, and here too, three or four years ago—but Paris is becoming so generally and impersonally large. Still, I can't imagine I won't succeed in finding the right thing, or something as close as possible to it (just trust me) — actually, wouldn't a boarding house also be worth considering, if one did not have to take all one's meals there? I look forward to making some pleasant discovery; Paris used to be just the place for this, and I used to think that *only* here was it possible to exchange a cherished image for reality without any loss. But even *here* realities no longer have the time to grow into their full-fledged kindly selves — You see I can't stop disparaging Paris — even the very Paris I want to make beautiful for you—

Rainer Maria

Monday, toward noon

You know, I think the whole post office must have felt it, this Yes I just wrote to you, like a small earthquake; surely no word was ever written like that with one of those poor driven work-horse pens of theirs — too bad you won't see it as I wrote it

119

down: Despite the alien pen, it was *my* "Yes," every inch *my Yes.*

Ah, but, precious dear, what, what can I quickly tell you against myself? What warning can I still give you? Look, I want to write you the way I normally would . . . Am I deceiving you *after all?* You imagine me to be cheerful, jubilant — You write: "Do you still recognize yourself?" — Yes, oh yes, I recognize myself still. Yesterday was such an evening. But I did not stand on the balcony of my exuberance, swinging flags—; I wasn't even inside, in the chambers of courage, looking out through the tall windows onto the clear paths of the future; oh sister, oh darling, I was deep down again in the dark cellars of my downcastness, down, down — and what I had held out above to fly in the storm was like a small tear-stained handkerchief in my hands.

Magda, perhaps you will feel, the moment you touch me, that the rift is irreparable after all—or that some alien dark hand rests somewhere against the curve of the bell, so that even the purest touch cannot resonate. Then *tell* me, heart. I will hardly feel any pain, only a kind of soundless relief, no disappointment at all, nor a return to an abandoned and half-forgotten painfulness: I still believe in *that* much more than in the unbelievable; and have evidence for it even unto my innermost blood. In the past, even two years ago, the call of a bird in the woods was all I needed to make me feel healthy, glad, strong, all the way from my soul to my willing body. How often since then have I been in the country, by the sea, face to face with the most potent forces, and was weary and gazed out, empty of any feeling except that I *couldn't.* — Tell yourself this, Magda, take it seriously, take it gravely into your heart, which is sacred to me, keep all your exit doors wide open behind you — I will not hold you back, my hands have long,

long ago promised themselves never to cling (nor did God make them for that purpose).

. . . [27]

The day after tomorrow, Magda. My first impulse was to leave *today*. Then I told myself: No. In this most generous event of my life I too should be generous—generous even toward time, toward everything that has yet to be settled and organized here, and be calmer, and full of composure. And so I wired you: Wednesday evening. And now go about my arrangements and dispositions and my packing: I want to be sure that I have everything, including books, whether for a short visit or a long one. In regard to finding a place for you to live here, I want to write a few letters and make one or two errands, by way of preparation; for it is much more difficult to get anything definite done by mail. And in the end, if one only had the faith, even *this* would be wonderful: not to hurry, not to barter for the extra day, but to quietly persist, in God's safekeeping, closer to you with each minute.

One more thing concerning the living arrangements — for years I've been in the habit of stopping, with diminishing delight, at the Hospiz des Westens, Marburgerstrasse 4 (near the Gedächtniskirche) — shall I do so this time? Or is there a suitable boarding-house in the Grunewald? Wire me about this as soon as you have this letter, please, but don't go to any trouble about it. I think the telegram will reach me here Wednesday in time for me to leave a forwarding address. If you don't send a telegram, I'll go to the Hospiz des W. — — — —

Magda!

Rainer

Rilke to Benvenuta

The weather's overtaking us: March storms. How they chase the rain clouds across the sky, scarcely leaving them time for raining; and suddenly everything opens up and an almost vacant, unprepared clarity sees itself reflected in the wet streets. And it's been that way all night. Do you know, sister, that I am afraid, *in the city,* during such nocturnal storms? Doesn't it look as if they ignored the city in their elemental pride? But a lonely country house, that they will see and embrace with their violent buffeting, hardening it — it even makes one want to go out into the roaring garden; at least one stands by the window in sympathy with the agitated old trees that behave as though the spirit of the prophets had taken possession of them. Glorious, isn't it—that we are so closely akin to all this and profoundly at one with it. That the pressure of our blood must constantly change in response to the counterpressure of the whole world, and behold, the body endures it, and the heart within is alone facing all the rest.

February 24, early morning

I find this sheet: and always I would go on to another, writing letter after letter, not one could have waited in the drawer even for an hour, dearest, they all rushed off toward you. But I see now that the world is still full of jealousy— which I have always been inclined to regard as the most obsolete of all passions, the one most worn-out in every respect. No sooner do I sit down at the table than my suitcase rebels, my

122

luggage, my baggage — whatever their collective designation may be, for there are several among which I must choose and decide (it's their turn again, they insist), yes, and I even agree with them, for they want to go to you; but, you see, *so do I;* for the time being, this paper is still my only poor and yet so splendid means, Magda, of being with you, of talking to you. Have I ever talked to a human being, dear heart, no, I don't know what I ever used to communicate with them, I just took off in their direction, I think I ran them over and then they'd lie there, dead, or else leap out of the way at the last moment, terrified, and I would just blindly drive on and on, circling the globe, thinking all the while that I was driving around inside that person, the one who had saved himself. Talking to you is not like ex-pressing oneself at all, it is a turning inward, it is an imperceptible growing, like the child moving inside the mother's womb.

I thought about this yesterday: how the most fleeting relation between people is governed by the state of mind they bring to it — how at once a vastness will enter into it if that vastness is there to begin with. Indeed it is impossible for one in whom this is at all alive to speak to a cabby without an unexpected gentleness arising between that cabby and himself, a happiness for each other, a sacrament. I had some hurried errands to do, everything was good, and the eyes I met with gave me an astonished reception, there was a readiness I found in people as in freshly turned spring soil. I was almost finished when I paid a visit to a young Frenchman, a poet who conducts a small trade in pictures on the rue de Seine in order to protect his own art from any sort of dubiousness; almost as though he could be sure that this sieve would catch all remnants of acquisitiveness and ulterior motive, to let only the purest thought enter the beautiful vessels of his simple poems. Ah, but in the end such sieves grow more and more clogged with everyday sediments! Love, I was able to give him such rich and warm solace, to speak to him with such conviction about some verses of his that I had recently read in a review, it was so deeply true, for in my heart there was nothing but truth. And do you know what happened when I entered: I saw him standing there, still at some distance, as if one could not get closer to him — mais — he said, mais ce moment j'avais pensé à vous, mais vous ne pouvez pas vous imaginer combien c'est étonnant — mais je pensais à vous tout à l'heure — mais c'est de la télépathie, mais est-ce que cela vous arrive quelque fois? Cela doit vous arriver . . . and it took a while before he had composed himself and sat facing me, still amazed, in his little cubicle. We had not seen one another since April of last year—this happens easily, given my reclusiveness here—and not exchanged any letters either, — and so the good man was struck to the core: his thinking of me, my stepping in. Imagine, I spoke to him of *you*. Yes, I described briefly the kind of room I am envisioning for you here — he knows many painters who come and go, so it might be possible to rent a studio, which would offer space and the greatest freedom for your piano.

This made it clear to me, love, how I have never been in the least secretive; whenever I had a secret, as a young man, I would reveal it; for I sensed people's suspicion — the moment one hid something, they would attach their worst thoughts to it. That tormented me, I wanted to anticipate them, show them how beautiful it was. Later my solitude had become so proverbial that some of my friends who wanted to help me did so precisely on account of my loneliness, so I too felt obligated to take them on a tour inside me from time to time, to cast a light into all the corners so they could see the sheer emptiness all around.

True, in my childhood I must have known of places within

me where one could store things that no one was supposed to find; in fact I believe most of my experience was secret, partly because it was altogether inexpressible, partly because there wasn't a person in my surroundings to whom one might have spontaneously imparted whatever *could* be expressed. Already during my military education,[28] where none of the outward circumstances could be brought into harmony with my nature, whose direction was already determined, I seem to have committed treason against my secrecy. To expose the incongruence of my inner conditions was the only counterweight I possessed against a world which crudely outweighed me on all sides, a world which everyone around me more or less gladly acknowledged as real and right, while I rebelled against it, denied it in all its manifestations, indeed was quite definitely obsessed with refuting it by means of other realities. When I come to think of it, I longed for a reality that would reduce the monstrous quotidian in which I was locked to a small, embarrassed, humiliated thing, a thing surpassed, indeed forced to hesitantly admit that it did not exist. Sometimes I expected such a reality to come from outside, from my family, who would suddenly turn out to occupy an utterly unsuspected high rank heretofore denied it; from some uncle who, through his connections to some great lord or the Emperor himself, would have a clarifying influence on my real position; again, from time to time it seemed to me that, strictly speaking, such intervention could only be expected of God, and then I felt a bond of trust between him and me, and had conversations with him in which, I am sure, I did not hold back with recommendations for bringing about the downfall of the military school. But as one grew warm with God in this urgent intercourse, the strangest, most incomprehensible thing happened: One could not win him over for any annihilation or degradation of the surrounding circumstances, for as soon as one started speaking to him, the military school was no longer there. Just as, in later life, one may become so powerfully absorbed in contemplation as to lose all sense of one's body except for an innermost point of existence from which one continues to act, inexhaustibly, out and beyond, so did the boy's need, by its instinctual attachment to the divine, transcend its own motives and become—outside, in space, as it were—a pure unconditional relation, an independent, magnificent experience of the soul. However much one ascribed to God the responsibility for such moments, the feeling that one could achieve them, that one could endure them, that one was instantly able to accept God's intentions, expanded one's own consciousness to new breadths, and it was on this basis that one eventually formed quite vague but infinitely grand expectations of oneself. And with these expectations there began a secrecy that was quite beyond one's powers to relinquish. Here one stood before one's heart, and the heart was closed, there was no cause for celebration of either the one or the other; but between this standing and that closedness there was an incomprehensible correspondence; the reticent silence of a law was in it, a life in abeyance, a future not yet arrived.

Wednesday morning, six o'clock

Magda, oh Magda, your visitor, how weak in courage he is, what a faint-heart. One who would like still to wait, struggle, stand there, prepare himself. Write to you. In letters, he could reach out to you with an inexhaustible soul — can he continue to do so? Love, if only I were like the little bird voice outside, simply admitting that day is breaking. It isn't excessively glad yet, this little urban bird voice in February, but if only I had that small ready sound with which it admits that day is allowed to come. Ah, I want to grow strong first and overcome some danger with you in my heart, and come to you only then. The way you sometimes felt you could see me, slender, and treading very lightly. Poor and threadbare, dear heart, I come to you, with all my yesterdays and all that remains impenetrable, with my whole defeat still clinging to me. I shall see you, Magda, with these unprepared eyes; my hands, my hands of yesterday, shall find refuge in yours — my heart shall feel your heart as little John inside Elizabeth felt little Jesus inside Mary—: but is it pure enough for such sudden joy? Tell me, what does one do on the day before such a day? How does one spend the night, to make the heart worthy? What if a dream comes and spoils me toward you, as happened just an hour ago, when you took me by the hand in a tall forest and led me away from the path I wanted to take: a narrow cleft in the forest, rising slightly between the solemn stems, the ground a metallic green from damp growing leaves; — farther above, in the middle of this path, blocking it, as it were, stood a single tall tree that did not branch out into a crown until it had long stood in silent composure — behind it, the glade continued to rise, but around the tree there was a faint golden misty radiance that soaked up the forest's interior—: This was the path I wanted to walk—but you overtook me on my left and took my hand and quickly, gently led me past it; at once I saw another direction, but I no longer know what it was like there. . . .

One thing I want to do the night before I see you, Benvenuta, is to wake and pray and kneel and be as sober as if I never needed nourishment — on all sides sustained by my expectation, by your imminence. — Ah but where in my past do I find the repose of childhood and the toughening exertions of youth, and how can I hope for the future to heal me, since I've already meddled with it long ago? A page, before he was knighted, would kneel in darkness at the precise point where the rays of those three powers intersected; this is why in that night the boys grew strong, transparent, imbued with futurity—: But I—when they would come for me in the morning, they would find me asleep in the chapel. Magda, I sometimes fear that I am one who has never learned to distinguish between hardness and softness; as though I felt nothing in either except their intensity, and lost them both, for there they resemble each other in feeling, like the burning of heat and the burning of cold.

In the train on the afternoon of the 26th[29]

Like the wind I passed through reed and bushes
and escaped from every house like smoke.
Others found their customary pleasures;
I, a foreign custom, kept my rule.
Clasped by others' hands, my hands took fright
as if entering a fateful compact;
all, by pouring themselves out, found increase;
I succeeded only in being spilled.

Just to gaze upon the stars above one
does require a foothold on the earth;
for all trusting only comes from trusting
and all giving is a gift returned.
Night, alas, asked nothing of me, ever.
But when I addressed the constellations,
injury facing the uninjurable,
What had I to stand on? Was I here?

Flooding toward me on this somber voyage,
I can feel the coursing of your heart.
Only hours remain before I gently

lay my hands into your gentle hands:
Oh how long since they have been at rest.
Can you imagine that for years I've traveled
thus: a stranger among other strangers?
Now at last you've come to take me home.

Thursday evening, before you come in

This is how I imagined my leaving Paris, a final hour there
dedicated to you, I writing by my lamp, writing to you, as if it
were just one of those many evenings; it didn't happen that
way. There were letters to write until the last moment, my
packing had taken an endless time—and then the people
came to fetch the luggage, the door stood open, the inquisitive
emptiness of the stairway rushed into the room and right
through me, truly as if I were no longer there. And yet—

*(At this moment I knocked and you said: "Yes?"—almost
anxiously—and then I stood in the room and we held each
other's hands.)**

---

* The last paragraph (in parentheses) is a postscript by Benvenuta.

Rilke and Benvenuta

A Commentary

by Joachim W. Storck

What sort of madness has come over me, how could I erupt like that? Even at night when I lie there without casting forth any fiery matter, it seems to me that the glow of my rebellious lava must hover above me as it does over Stromboli on its element-days.

—Rilke to Benevenuta,
February 17, 1914

Shortly after Rilke's death at the beginning of 1927, Rilke's friend the philosopher and essayist Rudolf Kassner wrote in his "Memories of Rilke," which appeared in the *Frankfurter Zeitung:* "The public will soon receive an overabundance of very beautiful letters which he bestowed on his friends. For many years his entire productivity consisted of writing such letters." This prediction has been richly borne out. Rilke today is recognized as one of the most prolific letter-writers of his time—a time when he already counted himself among those "old-fashioned people" who "still regard letter-writing as one of the most beautiful and productive means of social inter-course." After the first, rather inadequately selected and edited, collections of his letters appeared in the thirties, addi-tional carefully prepared editions of various correspondence were published and thoroughly analyzed by scholars; and the possibility of further publications in this vein is foreseeable. Without a doubt, letter-writing played a special role in Rilke's life and in his evolution as an artist. In his testament of 1925 Rilke expressly confirmed that "from certain years on," he had occasionally "channeled into letters . . . a portion of [his] nature's productivity." This passage seems to be an understatement, but it was in fact meant to legitimize later publication of his letters.

These remarks of Rilke reveal two different motives for writing letters that, in a certain sense, seem almost to cancel each other out. The characterization of letters as a "means of social intercourse" stresses their social function; the letter is supposed to maintain a relationship between two people through a dialogue; it remains incomplete until it is part of a correspondence. But, on the other hand, when a poet channels into his letters a portion of his "nature's productivity," the letters become a medium of his creativity, closely related to his actual poetic work. Here the monological, self-expressive aspect of letter-writing becomes evident, to which is added the further dimension of "factual telling," a major preoccupation of Rilke's, especially during his years in Paris.

In most of Rilke's letters, these ingredients are commingled, and the degree to which one or the other predominates is to a great extent determined by the person to whom they are addressed and by the nature of the relationship. As a letter-writer, Rilke had an extraordinary capacity for sensitively attuning himself to a wide variety of correspondents, which is perceptible even in the style, the tone, and the fluctuations of mood and temperament in his letters. But what happened when Rilke did not know the person to whom he was writing, if he conjured up that person from the letters he received and then filled in his vision with his own wishes, longings, and needs?

These were the conditions under which the correspondence with Benvenuta evolved: an outpouring of letters that gave rise within a few weeks to a mirror image of Rilke's personality, and that, at the same time, uncovered and elucidated the subtlest underlying sources and motives for his poetry.

How did these letters to Benvenuta come to be written? Letters that occupy a singular place in Rilke's legacy, letters written in the course of a single month yet substantial enough to fill a volume whose content Rilke regarded as the "testament" of his life? In order to adequately evaluate the significance of these letters in Rilke's life as well as in his development as a poet, one has to go back several years before they were written; back to the beginning of his personal epoch of crisis that began in 1910 with the completion of the novel he had written (for the most part) in Paris, *The Notebooks of Malte Laurids Brigge*, and that was prolonged by World War I. Rilke looked upon this interruption in his life as a watershed. In a long letter he wrote on December 28, 1911, from Duino, he confesses to his oldest and most constant friend, Lou Andreas-Salomé, that he had been left "quite like a survivor" in the wake of his book.

It was first of all a crisis in his creativity that Rilke was confessing to. It sprang to no small degree from his experience of that "terrible quality of art, which imposes upon one, the further one progresses in it, the obligation to reach to the utmost, the virtually impossible." In such times of crisis, Rilke, having lived alone for years in complete dedication to his work, longed for a new human relationship.

In a letter to Lou Andreas-Salomé, Rilke coins the word *Hinaussüchtigkeit* (roughly translatable as a "craving to get out"), which seems to contain all the dangers that threatened to overwhelm him again during the long intervals between the high points of his creative concentration.

The "craving to get out" as refuge or flight had many facets for Rilke during these years. He expressed it as a longing for communication, for an "understanding human being," as a need for a change of scenery, for new places to travel to, and, ultimately, in a greater urge to read. For years, travel was the most apparent and significant sign of this restlessness: several minor trips to Germany, to Bohemia, and to Italy, and those great voyages, each of which became an epoch during those years of "(inner and outer) unrest."

In the winter of 1912–13, Rilke traveled to Spain. After staying in Toledo, Cordoba, and Sevilla, he spent two months in the Spanish town of Ronda, "magnificently heaped on top of two enormous steep mountain ranges." That winter brought him several spontaneous poetic experiences that partially revived the initial creative surge he had felt at Duino shortly before the end of the year as a guest of his benefactress, the Princess Marie von Thurn und Taxis-Hohenlohe. But these few attempts remained fragmentary; they did not diminish his existential crisis nor the occasional doubts about his "calling."

The year 1913 was again marked by instability. Rilke traveled throughout Germany during the summer, and after returning to Paris in October, he reaffirmed his will "to remain as hidden as possible."

This constantly recurring motif of vacillation between the need for solitude and the "craving to get out" had its source in a particular biographical event. Rilke's "solitude," which was something he yearned for but which also oppressed him as soon as he wasn't "in the work," was in part due to financial pressure. For years, Rilke and his wife, the sculptor Clara Westhoff, had struggled separately to make progress in their respective arts after Rilke's family had cut off financial support to them. This led to an increasing estrangement between Rilke and his wife. In 1911, in the course of psychoanalysis, Clara

Westhoff realized her marriage could not be saved. She asked for a divorce, to which Rilke agreed. Due to various "external difficulties," Rilke and Clara Westhoff were never legally divorced; but in subsequent years their friendship continued.

In May 1913, after Rilke's return to Paris, he wrote a new poem that took up the motif of the "future beloved" in a slightly new vein. This time he is not addressing the imagined object of his unfulfilled longing but a spiritual and aesthetic phenomenon: music. In a peculiar way, the longing for the "unknown beloved" is interwoven with Rilke's sudden, previously unknown or anxiously avoided need to approach the realm of music. The *First Elegy* had already opened itself to the world of sound, receiving its "assignment" from a violin's devotion, attempting to listen to the "voices" as well as the "silence" and, finally, in remembrance of the "mourning for Linos," invoking the mythic origins of "venturing earliest music."

Several months later, at the end of 1913, Rilke began to realize that his longing could not be fulfilled; the "unknown beloved," in whose absence he "withers," became mythically transfigured into "the never arrived," whose imagined presence animates and, even in the movement of withdrawal, connects the images culled by Rilke from the flood of impressions impinging upon him.

On January 26, 1914, Rilke receives via the Insel Verlag a letter from a Viennese reader who identifies herself as Magda von Hattingberg and who, at "a time of inner disappointments" (a phrase that conceals the collapse of her first marriage), believes she has found a consoling voice in Rilke's *Stories of God*. In a perfectly spontaneous manner, she addresses Rilke, whom she has never met, as a "dear friend," and proceeds to thank him for the impression his youthful work has made on her, and for its influence on her music (she is a pianist)—"for you love music." Rilke immediately takes up "the rich tone" of her letter; it becomes his "own nature"; and he opens himself above all to the offer of music. The need he had felt of "receiving the world through a completely new sense" is now restimulated by this surprising letter from an unknown woman and in turn intensifies his receptivity for the subsequent letters he requests of her: "Don't let the new dear fire go out . . ."

Magda von Hattingberg's answer prompts Rilke to write a self-revealing letter that emerges from a veritable writing compulsion: "It is Sunday, I want to keep it holy by writing to you who now hold such a marvelous future for me in your hands . . ." In the third letter he exclaims that he would like "to write you in one sitting all the possible letters that could be written in a year." One quickly senses how in these letters the figure of his longing, which he had contained with difficulty in the formal structure of his poems—the "future one," the one "loved in advance"—is now virtually returning to life, embodied in this new correspondent.

A month earlier Rilke had expressed his desire for "the sisterly human being"; and now he calls the "unsuspected" friend his "sister, favorite sister in this unalloyed bliss . . ." In the sixth letter to Magda von Hattingberg he finally recognizes "the never arrived" as one who is arriving after all: "Oh my sister. Precious one, are you there, has God given you to me in the years of my life's anguish, that I may survive?"

And now, for the first time, he calls her Benvenuta, and soon after that, "Benvenuta, thou who hast come to me." A daily torrent of narrative, loving, and vacillating letters flows from Rilke's pen. This urgent pressure of an "inexhaustible communication" reminds one of that mythical figure he had invoked in his poem "Narcissus," the one with the "yielding center" and the "kernel full of weakness that does not hold the flesh of its fruit." In a way, this poetic image corresponds to the inner course of Rilke's letters to Benvenuta. In her mirroring presence, Rilke's thoughts attain their purity; she makes real all that he is thinking: "The words come like the first heavy drops from the wine-press of my memory." Rilke addresses the life of his friend as if he were "speaking to the clouds and the depths of my sky to discuss when and where to supply my nature with showers and clear weather." Indeed he feels as if in her heart he could for the first time express to God that he knows him.

Such letters then are, in part, monologues. And the letters he wrote day by day are virtually journals. When Rilke realizes, in the middle of a letter he has been writing for four days, that these messages are "monsters," no longer letters but "letter-titans in revolt against the gods of our hours," he decides to return to "work."

It is understandable that a question and a simultaneous realization should arise in Rilke's mind: "Tell me, once all this is written—will I live then, will I die? For this is the testament of all my past and future existence." And he adds the qualifying and self-critical question: "And who am I that I should be permitted to write it down with a heaving heart, addressing it to you, and seal it with your heart?" Has he not—and this secret reproach appears in various colorations elsewhere in the correspondence—in a sense violated Benvenuta's reality with the force of his own imagination, merely clouding "with many words" the joy with which she so purely approached him?·

This question, however, does not do justice to the problematic experience underlying the correspondence. That experience was grounded in Rilke's concrete longing for the "sisterly human being," for the "future beloved." What Rilke wanted his "letter-titans" to accomplish was, above all, that they convey all the many and conflicting levels of his nature. Rilke believed that with this written testament of his pure exaltation, with this contemplation of his nature, he would be able to bring about "an almost unsurpassable closeness."

But in attempting this he asked too much of the medium of letters, as at the beginning of the letter of February 16:

> Precious girl, I continue writing, addressing to your heart this incomprehensible journal of my desire to live — I feel as if this were my final, definitive work, to make myself true to you, true, do you hear, not likable — adamantly true — as if in your heart I might, for the first time, make myself plain to God, so that he would know me . . .

Rilke's attempt "to get a more human and natural footing in life" through his relationship with Benvenuta was doomed to fail. "Three (unachieved) months of reality" turned a "wonderful future" into something "foolishly hoped for."

July 1914, when Rilke sealed in an envelope the letters he had received from Magda von Hattingberg during the winter, must also have been the date of a piece of writing titled "Dernière lettre à B.," which Benvenuta received together with her later letters soon after Rilke's death. She divulged a portion of its contents in her *Buch des Dankes,* first published in 1943. It contains, in addition to the confession that "a great deal was buried and almost ceased to be expressible," a carefully worded indication of the artistic and suprapersonal nature of this epistolary "journal":

> . . . but if some day the hour of which you speak should come (and then it will be certain that I could not do otherwise than boundlessly affirm it), then testify that you are entitled to bear witness, since you bear the testament of my life in your blessed hands.

* * * *

The letters Rilke wrote to Benvenuta between January 26 and February 26, 1914, were aimed at a definite objective: the personal encounter, yearned for despite all the hesitations and finally agreed upon in the last letters. Magda von Hattingberg, née Reichling, had left her native city of Vienna in the middle of February 1914 to visit friends and her music teacher, Ferruccio Busoni, in Berlin. This city, then, was to be the site of Rilke and Benvenuta's first meeting and the point of departure for a voyage they would take together. And in fact it was there that the "three (unachieved) months of reality," which Rilke would later so bitterly lament, began.

Rilke had left Paris—and with it the studio he had rented for the entire winter—on February 26, 1914. Benvenuta's entry into his hotel room that evening brought the series of his letters to an abrupt end.

Our knowledge of the following weeks is based on two sources: Magda von Hattingberg's memoir, *Rilke und Benvenuta,* and a few isolated letters of Rilke's. All of the latter must be consulted, since the reliability of Benvenuta's *Buch des Dankes* is in dispute. This is due to the fact that Magda von Hattingberg does not cite Rilke's letters as letters but instead arbitrarily employs them to reconstruct her conversations with him.

Their first days in Berlin appear to have been the happiest for the two friends, who were still tentative and shy toward one another; these days were filled with the immediate experience of music the pianist was able to convey to the poet—an experience he was quite open to at first and that also led to a valuable meeting with the composer Busoni.

On March 9, Rilke wrote to Lou Andreas-Salomé of "the strangest turns of fate, and music—the most glorious music, through Busoni." He continued: "All sorts of unexpected, good things drew me here, I am staying until tomorrow, then going for a few days to Munich, Hotel Marienbad."

A few days after the trip to Munich, on March 12, Rilke wrote a detailed letter to the Princess Taxis, ending with a request for an invitation to Duino castle as soon as possible "to bring you a dear person who is important to my life, so that you may come to know her."

From March 20 to 26, Rilke and Benvenuta continued traveling via Innsbruck, Zurich, Winterthur, and Basel to Paris. On April 2 Rilke wrote to Sidonie Nadherny von Borutin that he had returned to "strongly neglected correspondence and work." On April 7, from Paris, he confirms that he and Benvenuta will visit the Princess Taxis in Duino. But now Rilke's letter takes on a peculiarly ambivalent tone: ". . . of course a great many things are coming together; if it were not *you,* no one would see his way clear in this; but I am confident that you will perceive what order there is in it, if indeed there is any to be found at all."

From April 20 until May 4 Rilke and Benvenuta lived in Duino. The princess, an understanding, motherly friend, very quickly recognized the nature of the situation in which Rilke was unable to see any "order." At the beginning of May, they traveled to Venice in the company of the princess and there they parted. "Benvenuta," too, had become the "never arrived" and proved to be "the one loved in advance." It was Magda who was left behind.

After spending two solitary weeks in Assisi, his chosen place of refuge—from where Rilke complained to the princess in Duino that "every atom" in his body was made "of a heavy blunt dullness"—Rilke returned to his abandoned studio in Paris and, finding himself once again bereft of funds, turned to his publisher Anton Kippenberg. His letter of May 26 conveys, despite all its reserve, a telling summary of the most recent chapter of his life, now shrunk to a mere episode after the most extraordinary exaltations:

> . . . I have drawn a thick line beneath the turbulent, unexpected last months, which might have brought an indescribable goodness—under certain circumstances—and now the fact that they have not brought it will have to be honestly understood and evaluated, and in the end an even purer usefulness will arise from it than could have come from all that was foolishly hoped for.

Such an understatement and veiled confession could be sent to a relative stranger but not to his oldest friend, Lou Andreas-Salomé. After a few days of meditation and recollection, Rilke wrote her another long letter on June 8 and 9 that contained, by way of self-accusation and self-analysis, the essential résumé of the Benvenuta experience, from both an existential and an artistic point of view. Significantly, he distinguishes between the biographical and the epistolary event.

In the second part of the letter Rilke gives us a glimpse of the significance the correspondence with Benvenuta had in bringing about the "turning point" he wished for and eventually brought to poetic fruition:

> What finally ended with such a perfectly miserable outcome for me began with many letters, easy, beautiful ones that sprang from my heart. . . . and if ever a deeply troubled person can become pure, I became so in those letters. The everyday and my relationship to it became to me in an indescribable fashion sacred and responsible—and thence a strong confidence seized me, as if now at last I had found the way out of the inertia of being dragged along by a constant fortuitousness. . . . so that for the first time I seemed to become the owner of my life, not by interpretive appropriation, exploitation and understand-

ing of what had been, but simply by that new truthfulness itself
which flowed through my memories as well.

ৡ

One of the world's foremost Rilke authorities, Joachim W.
Storck has lectured at Cambridge University and taught at the
universities of Frieburg and Marburg. Since 1971 he has been
responsible for the Rilke Archive at the Schiller-National-
museum/Deutsches Literaturarchiv in West Germany. In 1974
Dr. Storck became vice-president of the International Rilke
Society, and he is a founding member of the Fondation Rainer
Maria Rilke in Sierre, Switzerland. He is currently preparing a
two-volume edition of Rilke's *Letters on Politics*.

Notes
from the German Edition

1. Ellen Key (1849–1926), Swedish author and feminist, wrote an essay on Rilke in 1904 that appeared in her book *Seelen und Werke* in 1911. Rilke found himself generously but inaccurately portrayed by her. Ellen Key had invited him to Borgeby-Gard (Sweden), where Rilke spent the summer of 1904, and to Furnborg near Göteborg, where he lived in the fall of 1904. Their friendship came to an end in 1906. Cf. letters to Clara Rilke, June 14 and 21, 1906, and letter to Lou Andreas-Salomé, December 28, 1911.

2. Southern Spain: The "little Spanish town" of Ronda, where Rilke spent the winter of 1912–13.

3. *Amenophis IV* (Akhenaten), Egyptian Pharaoh, religious reformer, 1375–58 B.C. Portrait head from Tell el Amarna in the Altes Museum, Berlin.

4. The sphinx and the owl: This experience eventually found its poetic crystallization in the Tenth Elegy: ". . . But her gaze/ startles an owl from behind the crown's rim. And the bird,/ in a slow, skimming glide, brushes the cheek,/ the one with the ripest curve,/ and softly draws on the open double page of the dead's newborn hearing/ the indescribable outline."

5. Existence of pianos: Cf. Rilke's letter to the Princess Marie von Thurn und Taxis, April 10, 1913, and her answer of April 14, 1913.

6. Slave in the marketplace: Rilke had already used this image in the second part of the Spanish Trilogy (*Gedichte 1906–1926,* p. 103).

7. Marcel Proust (1871–1922), French novelist. *Du côté de chez Swann,* Paris, 1913.

8. Voyage on another continent: Rilke is referring to his North African sojourn (Algiers, Tunis, Egypt) in the winter of 1910–11. The Tunisian city is probably Kairouan (cf. letter to Lou Andreas-Salomé of March 16, 1912).

9. In Schmargendorf, Villa Waldfrieden: Rilke lived there from 1898–1900.

10. Three pictures: Amateur photos from Bad Rippoldsau, Schwarzwald, a spa Rilke visited in June 1913.

11. Daguerreotype of my father: Cf. the poem "Portrait of my father as a youth" (*Neue Gedichte*): ". . . You slowly vanishing Daguerreotype / in my more slowly vanishing hands."

12. "Unending is my amazement": Two distichs, lyrical fragment, Ronda, winter 1912–13 (*Gedichte 1906–1926,* p. 217.)

13. Rome: The "small house" is a garden house in the park of the Villa Strohl-Fern, where Rilke lived in the spring of 1904.

14. Five lines were omitted at the editor's request.

15. Eleonora Duse: Rilke had made the acquaintance of the great actress in Venice in 1912. He wrote several letters to influential theater people urging them to found a special theater for Duse, without success. The deep impression the actress made on Rilke is documented in numerous letters and reported conversations. Even before meeting her, he had celebrated her art in the poem "Bildnis" ("Portrait") (*Der Neuen Gedichte anderer Teil*) and in *"The Notebooks of Malte Laurids Brigge."*

16. Clara Rilke, née Westhoff: Sculptor, student of Rodin. Rilke had married her in 1901, lived with her until 1902 in Worpswede near Bremen, 1902–05 in Paris, 1904 in Rome, 1905 in Worpswede again, 1908 again in Paris, July–August 1910 in Oberneuland near Bremen, October 1912 and September 1913 in Munich. On October 31, 1913, Rilke had written to Princess Marie von Thurn and Taxis: "If I can (?), I will (?) let the divorce proceedings take their course this winter."

17. Two pages were omitted on the editor's request.

18. Marcel Proust: "A comment in the front." Rilke's note on the fly-leaf of the volume went as follows:

> . . . comme si ces milliers de choses dont chacune pourtant aurait eu envie de devenir un élément de cette vie, n'eussent point été employ-ées à le former; elles sont restées intactes — et un jour celui qui les retrouve, en fait une collection de souvenirs, avec tout le zèle d'un collectionneur acharné. Il ne néglige rien; ne rien préférer serait une qualité de l'artiste, pour laisser à l'âme toute la liberté de ses préférences innées la moindre chose de par elle peut être apparentée

aux évènements essentiels; mais ici il n'y a lien commun entre les faits, les remarques, les souvenirs que ce qui relie entre eux les objets d'une collection: qu'elle soit, autant que possible, complète.

19. Rudolf Kassner, aphorisms: *Aus den Sätzen des Yoghi,* Neue Rundschau 1911, vol 1. The aphorism Rilke wrote down from memory in Cairo (as he wrote to Kassner on June 16, 1911) was worded a little differently in the original: "Whoever wants to rise from inwardness [*Innigkeit*] to greatness must sacrifice himself." Rilke used his version of this sentence as an epigraph for the poem "Wendung" (Turning Point), written in June, 1914. — His new book: Rudolf Kassner, *Die Chimäre. Der Aussätzige,* Leipzig, Insel Verlag, 1914.

20. . . . unfair to C. R.: Refers to the two pages omitted on p. 64. (See note 17.)

21. Nine lines of this letter were omitted at the editor's request.

22. Vautrin: A character in Balzac's play *Vautrin,* and in his novel, *La dernière incarnation de Vautrin.* He is a cynical immoralist.

23. Herr von Schlözer: Leopold von Schlözer, who later wrote two books about Rilke, *Erinnerungen an Rilke* and *Rilke auf Capri.* Letters of his great uncle: *Römische Briefe von Kurt von Schlözer 1864–1869,* Stuttgart, 1912.

24. " . . . last passages of Malte Laurids": *The Notebooks of Malte Laurids Brigge* was completed in the Hotel Biron in Paris in January 1910.

25. Psychoanalysis: The "close friend" was Dr. phil. Victor Emil Freiherr von Gebsattel, born in 1883, who had known Rilke since 1908. This passage confirms the speculations of Ernst Pfeiffer in his well-informed notes on Rilke's correspondence with Lou Andreas-Salomé: that Rilke did not learn of psychoanalysis through Lou Andreas-Salomé but earlier (already in 1910!), through Gebsattel.

Dr. Poul Bjerre was the Swedish psychotherapist from whom Lou Andreas-Salomé (according to Pfeiffer) received her first detailed knowledge of Freud's theory. In response to a perplexed letter Rilke had written her on January 24, 1912, she urgently advised him not to undergo a psychoanalytic treatment. Thereupon Rilke wrote his famous letter of refusal to Gebsattel: ". . . to the extent that I know myself, I am sure that if my devils were exorcized, my angels, too, would be given a small, a very small (let's say) fright — and—please understand this—I cannot let this happen at any price." In October of the same year, during a stay in Munich, Rilke again met Gebsattel, who had analyzed Clara Rilke. On that occasion, he was once more confronted with the question. To avoid having to make a positive decision, Rilke departed for Spain.

It is worth noting that for years after, he showed a continued interest, indeed sympathy, for the new form of therapy. Several commentators have pointed out that the Third Elegy, for instance, could not have been written without this theoretical foundation.

26. The passage refers to Rilke's stay in the house of Alice Fahndrich, with Julie Freifrau von Nordeck zur Rabenau ("Frau Nonna") and Countess Manon zu Solms-Laubach. Cf. letter to Julie Freifrau von Nordeck zur Rabenau of January 2, 1912 (*Briefe 1907–1914,* pp. 152–55) and letter to Lou Andreas-Salomé of January 10, 1912.

27. Fifteen lines of this letter were omitted on the editor's request.

28. Military education: René Maria Rilke, whose father expected him to pursue a career as an officer, was a student at the Militär-Unterrealschule St. Pölten from September 1886 to June 1890, and at the Militär-Oberrealschule Mährisch-Weissenkirchen from September 1890 to May 1891.

29. In the train: The three stanzas of this poem were composed and written down in the inverse order. They are here transposed, as they are in the *Buch des Dankes,* in accord with the poet's oral instructions. Cf. *Gedichte 1906–1926,* p. 336.

Sources

Rainer Maria Rilke, *Gedichte 1906–1928,* Insel Verlag 1953.

Rainer Maria Rilke und Lou Andreas-Salomé. Briefwechsel, Insel Verlag 1951.

Rainer Maria Rilke and Marie von Thurn und Taxis. Briefwechsel, Insel Verlag 1951.

Rainer Maria Rilke, *Briefe 1906–1907,* Insel Verlag 1930.

Rainer Maria Rilke, *Briefe 1907–1914,* Insel Verlag 1933.